Humane Insight

THE NEW BLACK STUDIES SERIES

Edited by Darlene Clark Hine and Dwight A. McBride

A list of books in the series appears at the end of this book.

Humane Insight

Looking at Images of African American Suffering and Death

COURTNEY R. BAKER

UNIVERSITY OF ILLINOIS PRESS
Urbana, Chicago, and Springfield

An earlier version of chapter 3 was previously published
as "Emmett Till, Justice, and the Task of Recognition,"
Journal of American Culture 29, no. 2 (2006): 111–24.
Reprinted by permission from Blackwell Publishing.

First Illinois paperback, 2017

1 2 3 4 5 C P 5 4 3 2 1
∞ This book is printed on acid-free paper.

The Library of Congress cataloged the cloth edition as follows:
Baker, Courtney.
Humane insight : looking at images of African American
suffering and death / Courtney R. Baker.
pages cm. — (The new Black studies series)
Includes bibliographical references and index.
ISBN 978-0-252-03948-5 (cloth : alk. paper)
ISBN 978-0-252-09759-1 (e-book)
1. African Americans—Violence against—History—Pictorial
works. 2. African Americans—Social conditions—Pictorial
works. 3. Documentary photography—Social aspects—United
States—History. 4. Photojournalism—Social aspects—United
States—History. 5. Empathy—Social aspects—United States—
History. 6. Racism—United States—History—20th century.
I. Title.
E185.61.B148 2015
305.896'0730222—DC23 2015003808

PAPERBACK ISBN 978-0-252-08299-3

In Memory of

Thomas Cary Saunders

1919–2008

and

Dorothy Belle Ottley Saunders

1921–2013

Contents

Acknowledgments

In September 2001, I watched via television as a space that I had traversed and a place that I recognized became permanently disfigured. Since then, I have sought to understand what compelled me to watch those extraordinary images of people dying and, more, to appreciate what I learned from watching other human beings in despair and death. In terms of its sheer horror, 9/11 represented a scenario that has been repeated throughout time and throughout the world and one that will sadly but I fear inevitably be repeated in the future. No discussion of global capitalism, non-statist military syndicates, or mobilized rhetoric has enabled me to understand fully the extraordinary images of people of myriad races, ethnicities, and nationalities dying. I still struggle to understand the magnitude of 9/11 and of other events wherein humanity has been laid to waste. In the wake of that day, it was the image and the word—a specific image and particular words, actually—through which I came to recognize the struggle for comprehension to be itself a worthy object of study.

A few months after the destruction of the World Trade Center, I revisited the first words of Michel de Certeau's essay "Walking in the City": "Seeing Manhattan from the 110th floor of the World Trade Center."[1] As it happened, I *had* seen the city from the point of view that Certeau described, but I now knew, as the text certainly did not or could not, that this point of view could never now be replicated. The tense of the verb *seeing* now signaled to me a remarkable lack of hubris. Did the destruction of the location invalidate the knowledge Certeau was imparting? To speak metaphorically, did the sermon die when the mount crumbled?

On the contrary: Certeau's observations on visual knowledge and hubris became more poignant through the destruction of his former observation post. For indeed, in the book in which the essay appears, *The Practice of Everyday Life,* Certeau questions the security, stability, and "voluptuous pleasure" of the God's-eye view of the modern city, asking, "To what erotics of knowledge does the ecstasy of reading such a cosmos belong?"[2] To aspire to such heights of knowledge at such a vast remove from the object of knowledge itself—the city—is truly to mimic Icarus and delight in "the fiction of knowledge . . . [as] a viewpoint and nothing more."[3] And so, Certeau predicts from his post on the 110th floor of the World Trade Center an uninvested view of humanity that would precipitate the inevitable "Icarian fall."[4]

The current project finds enormous wisdom in this hubristic resistance to such an uninvested view of humanity. The encounter with human beings and embeddedness in the world are what educates us in the humanity of ourselves and of others. Certainly, Mamie Till-Mobley understood this innately. As she looked upon the destruction wrought by white racists upon the now-dead, now-deformed body of her son Emmett in a Chicago mortuary in 1955, Till-Mobley recognized—and then mobilized—the entwined knowledge of her suffering and that of her son. Until I understood this, looking at Emmett Till's photo was something that I sought to avoid with precisely placed Post-it notes in my books. And yet the photographs were created so that I would have to look and to reckon with the way the image unsettled me. The visual encounter with the image of death and suffering, it appeared, brought on the crucial education about the self and of what it means to be human. It is an education founded upon hubris and vulnerability. The current study identifies in the visual encounter a collapsing, a falling of the self into the reality of the other. It is a reality that is only made legible through the discourse of humanity. I could not have achieved this education alone. I thank Certeau and Till-Mobley for starting it.

There are many more to thank for helping me narrate the intellectual journey contained in these pages. This book would never have encountered its readers without the perseverance of my editor at the University of Illinois Press, Dawn Durante, and the faith of acquisitions editor Larin MacLaughlin and the New Black Studies series editors Darlene Clark Hine and Dwight A. McBride. My anonymous readers were diligent, providing me with wonderful insights and the best gift for which a scholar could wish: to be taken seriously.

I am grateful daily for the opportunity for graduate study in the Literature program at Duke University. Learning amid friends and fellow students turned colleagues—among them Erica Edwards, Rebecca Wanzo—and the faculty turned colleagues and friends—Ian Baucom, Grant Farred, Jane Gaines, Avery Gordon, Wahneema Lubiano, Negar Mottahedeh, Richard Powell, Jan Radway, Maurice Wallace, Susan Willis—seems truly Edenic to me now. The connections from that place and time have served me well, leading my writing into the able editorial hands of Erika Stevens who often steered me straight as I edited this manuscript. Duke also introduced me to the generous and dear friend, colleague, mentor, and super-scholar-hero Leigh Raiford who has come to my aid and inspired me too many times to mention.

Simon Hay helped me cross the bridge from graduate student life to tenure-track faculty life by being present in both places. I simply cannot imagine my first years at Connecticut College without the love of him and Cybèle Locke and their amazing sons, Gabriel and Fred. I am grateful for the support I received for this work from Connecticut College in the form of funding (from the R. F. Johnson Faculty Development Fund, the Hodgkins Untenured Faculty Development Fund, and the Research Matters award) and in the shape of colleagues like Blanche Boyd, Jim Downs, Leo Garofola, David Kim, Nina Martin, Julie Rivkin, Mab Segrest, Chris Steiner, and Lina Wilder. The college's Center for the Critical Study of Race and Ethnicity continues to provide the ballast for my scholarship. Film Studies and my home department of English have provided me with the space to explore topics of interest and to indulge my expertise. My former students Kolton Harris and Will Shadbolt conducted excellent research for parts of this book, and I am thankful for their careful work.

I and this project have happily found intellectual sustenance beyond the boundaries of my home institution. The New Orleans Historical Society helped me answer questions I did not think possible to resolve. My year in the English Department at Denison University, supported by the Consortium for a Strong Minority Presence at Liberal Arts Colleges, allowed me to make great strides and to explore my project in a classroom with wonderful, eager students. I am especially grateful to Linda Krumholz for nurturing me during my time there. I thank, too, the Yale colleagues—Jacqueline Goldsby, John Mackay, Caleb Smith, and Laura Wexler—who have kindly opened their minds, homes, and hearts to me. Koritha Mitchell continues to inspire me with her intellect and her long-distance running skills. Michael Gillespie fulfills my desperate need to discuss black film. Michael Belleisles is a fearless and righteous scholar who pulled from nowhere the time to help me get my history right. Daphne Brooks, fearless in her own way, has helped me more than she knows. Those who I know only through their work (and on Facebook) bear acknowledging here as well for their great contributions to academia and to my own scholarship: Maurice Berger, Farah Jasmine Griffith, Saidiya Hartman, Kara Keeling, Elaine Scarry, and Shawn Michelle Smith.

Friends and family have sustained me through this (sometimes hair-pulling) process. Lucky for me, some of these important folks are also colleagues and are identified above. I would be nowhere (or maybe someplace crying) without the affection and fine-feeling of Jennifer Mellon and Elise Dunphe. Jarita Davis thoughtfully invited me to speak in her lovely corner of the Northeast. Lucretia Baskin has listened to me grumble during the hard parts of my trek into academia and consistently offered sound advice and a willing ear. Andrew Benner, with his genius and kindness and care, has made the last part of this book process and everything else in my life immeasurably better.

I lost two very important members of my family in the process of writing the book. My grandparents, Thomas Saunders and Dorothy Ottley Saunders, were intoxicatingly beautiful blends of kindness, strength, and the purest love. I miss them both, tremendously. The journey was improved, however, by the addition of my nephew Noah Baker and the willingness of his parents, Gregory Baker and Jenelle DeCoteau, to share his joyfulness with me. My parents, Howard Baker and Carolyn Saunders Baker, have put such faith in me and celebrated me that "thank you" seems not quite to cover it.

It seems to me that a book about suffering and death would be lacking if it did not contain an acknowledgment of the reality of suffering and death. To all who are in this book, to all who are connected to someone or to some event in this book, to those who have survived and those who have fallen: May your suffering not be in vain. May it lead us toward knowledge for better lives to come.

Humane Insight

Introduction

Those of us who have witnessed in person or at a distance even a few of the cruel scenarios of famine, disaster, and bloodshed have likely questioned what we are to "do" with what we have seen. Most of us have at some time questioned our permission to look at another person's pain. Some of us have looked and then dedicated ourselves to ensuring that such scenes will not appear again. Others have rushed into the very scenes that initially shocked us and worked hand in hand with the people whose suffering moved us. Still others of us have looked away, too horrified by the pain and suffering on display to bear in our minds these awful images. And of course there are those who endured the suffering themselves, who testified to their personal knowledge of its horror and threat to their very existence. And there are those, too, who could not testify at all, but whose bodies are nevertheless called upon to tell the tale of their demise and to move those who did survive toward justice.

We who look from a safe distance at the pain and death of others have been challenged by the motivations and exploitations that are involved in this peculiar visual dynamic. There are troubling consequences set up by this looking scenario in which a spectator seems to hold power over an exposed victim. Scholars in fields of visual analysis—art, photography, film—have identified these power games of the ocular kind as invoking imperialist and imperious attitudes. The term *gaze* has come to name the dangerous look that targets and immobilizes its human objects in webs of racism, sexism, and other debilitating beliefs. But not all looks are gazes. *Looking* is a more variegated practice and even bears the potential for positive change. Our discussions of the *look* as opposed to the *gaze* have been stymied by the look's flexibility—an inconsistency that has been and can continue to be a principle for more ethical human interactions.

The act of looking at the pain of another has by turns been accused of violence and aligned with bravery. One of the most significant questioners of the ethics of beholding atrocity has been Susan Sontag who, in two volumes—the landmark *On Photography* (1977) and her final book, *Regarding the Pain of Others* (2003)—elaborates on her discomfort with the recurrent spectacle of pain and suffering made possible by the photographic medium. In the latter work, Sontag speculates that "[p]erhaps the only people with the right to look at images of suffering of this extreme order are those who could do something to alleviate it . . . or those who could learn from it. The rest of us are voyeurs, whether or not we mean to be."[1] This seems to be a shockingly restrictive gesture in its evocation of exclusive rights and its alignment of "the rest of us" with the denigrated class of voyeurs. In day-to-day experience, by contrast, looking is far more promiscuous than depicted here, and looking at suffering does not result in being measured by its returns, however valuable and idealized the function of alleviating of pain might be. Yet learning from looking, despite the rather short shrift it is given in Sontag's passage, has and continues to be a compelling project for the eradication of injustice worldwide. As Sharon Sliwinski has offered in a useful counter to Sontag's estimation, "[t]he history of human rights—and the history of their abuse—is a richly illustrated one" attended by spectators in whose minds "the ideal of a shared humanity literally comes into view."[2] Although one can, as Sontag maintains, look at suffering and see nothing of note, a more favorable response and certainly one worth noting is one in which the look moves and instructs the viewer on humanity's greatest lesson—the value of human life.

To the extent that vision is a key sense through which human beings come to understand and appreciate the existence of other human subjects, we can reasonably and responsibly discuss how multiple media forms attempt to approximate this primary and immediate encounter between looking subjects and visible bodies. Certainly, the intervention of specific techniques (such as painting) and technologies (such as photography) into what I am characterizing as a sort of primal scene of intersubjective encounter recommends acknowledgment of the specific contours of mediated visual encounter. Nonetheless, to the extent that this project is concerned with the core scenario in which a subject's vision inspires awareness of another's subjectivity, the current book insists upon a transmedia discussion of the look that underwrites all mediated encounters. What proceeds from this investment and follows in these pages is therefore a preference for a phenomenological rather than a materialist assessment of the look. In other words, lest it be mistaken, this study's interrogations of visual encounters with the Other through drawings and films, as well as in the flesh, should not be read as avoiding the nuances of these myriad mediations, but instead as a much-needed return to the fundamental sensation—sight—and the core belief—that the self is not the only conscious subject—upon which all visual innovations are based.

The worries expressed by Sontag and her followers about the effects of beholding visualizations of violence and destruction are premised, after all, not on the particular medium, but on the human capacity of visual apprehension. Furthermore, we need not, I insist, assume that "[t]o photograph people is to violate them, by seeing them as they never see themselves, by having knowledge of them that they can never have."[3] This claim of Sontag's from her earlier work on photography rather overstates the case, locating in a particular medium rather than in the act of intersubjective looking itself a potentially violent discursive gesture. Indeed, is not the risk of an ossifying imperialist look—the gaze, in other words—precisely what haunts psychoanalyst and race theorist Frantz Fanon in the echoing phrase "Look, a Negro!"—a declaration uttered in his presence, not with respect to a photograph? This key phrase that underscores vision's vexed contributions to Fanon's interest in the "Fact of Blackness" is sharpened to its most harmful point when the young white French girl embellishes this observation and cries *in Fanon's presence,* "Mama, see the Negro! I'm frightened!"[4] It is by restoring the problem of visualizing the Other to the human body and its sense of sight that we might fulfill Fanon's poignant prayer—"O my body, make of me always a man who questions!"[5]

Moments in which this questioning is foreclosed and interest in the livelihood and dignity of the Other is absent are important ideological moments to which we must attend. African Americanist historian Saidiya Hartman addresses these resistant looks in her examination of the spectacle of enslaved blacks and the white audiences that looked upon them. The enslaved black body was made to dehumanize itself not only through the denial of pain but also through performances of pleasure. Expressions of pain were either ignored or dismissed as deceptive simulacra by those who held the power to transform those conditions. If the slave is not human, the logic runs, he cannot experience pain as a human, thereby eliminating the need or responsibil ity of onlookers to recognize those bodies as like their own. Underwriting the resistance to the perception of the black slave's humanity is the fact that "pain provides the common language of humanity; it extends humanity to the dispossessed and, in turn, remedies the indifference of the callous."[6] Pain, then, can enable the materialization of an immaterial humanity that lies beyond linguistic representation. Viewed in this way, pain becomes the currency of black liberation from injustice and state-sanctioned violence. One sees here the logic that motivated the writing of several sentimental slave narratives: if only my pain is recognized by my oppressors, then I will be free.

This moralist mobilizing of pain and suffering is paramount in the aesthetics of sentimentalism. In the Western literary tradition, sentimentalism's refinement into a style meant ascribing to pain a value in a moral economy, a facet highlighted by the alternative title of the foundational and archetypal novel of the sentimental genre: *Pamela, or Virtue Rewarded* (1740). Sentimental nineteenth-century American antislavery narratives would also seek rewards for their virtuous characters who often suffered not only under the yoke of womanhood (like the eponymous Pamela) but also under that of blackness. Sentimental black female characters like Harriet Wilson's Frado (*Our Nig* [1859]), Harriet Jacobs's pseudonymous Linda Brent (*Incidents in the Life of a Slave Girl* [1861]), and Harriet Beecher Stowe's Eliza (*Uncle Tom's Cabin* [1852]) figured in scenes of suffering meant to effect, if not the actual liberation of real black women, the moral redemption of black women suffering under conditions created by the institution of racialized enslavement.

The sentimental appeal for black liberation has not been limited to women or to the literary medium. As is discussed in the first chapter of this book, through speech and spectacle (in person and in photographs), black men recruited the image of their bodies' wounding under slavery both to illustrate slavery's injustice and to advocate for restoration of virtue—what we might well construe here as "humanity"—to an enslaved black American populace.

Appeals to sentiment through the presentation of pain have been crucial to progressive black movements in America well beyond the abolition of slavery. The clamor for freedom and the recognition of humanity observed in the preemancipation era extend well beyond that moment, echoing resoundingly in the antilynching campaigns and the civil rights movement of the twentieth century. Indeed, we can observe throughout these eras a rhetoric of black liberation premised upon the ethical beholding of the black body's physical sensation. This book charts that rhetorical thread as it has been invoked by what Elizabeth Alexander, in her discussion of how spectacles of violence cohere an African American community, calls "contemporary sites of conflict."[7]

This kind of looking, one in which the onlooker's ethics are addressed by the spectacle of others' embodied suffering, is what I am calling in this book *humane insight.* Whereas the gaze ignores or denies the humanity of the person being looked at, humane insight seeks knowledge about the humanity of that person. It is an ethics-based look that imagines the body that is seen to merit the protections due to all human bodies. Humane insight describes a decision to identify the body being looked at as a human body, a gesture that is integral to the formation of our social interactions. It is a look that turns a benevolent eye, recognizes violations of human dignity, and bestows or articulates the desire for actual protection.

The gesture of identifying the Other as possessing humanity and deserving the bodily protections that comes with that quality is radically overthrown in the perpetration of physical violence against another body. Elaine Scarry explains that the torturer, whose sole occupation is the infliction of pain on another, must deny the victim's humanity in order to proceed. The torturer's ignoring the victim's pain, often powerfully expressed by cries and pleading, is itself a form of torture as it violently demonstrates to the victim not only an absence of compassion but also an absence of successful communication. The communication of pain is frustrated by more than the torturer's unwillingness to acknowledge it. Pain itself resists its expression by invalidating the verifications of language and consciousness themselves. Pain throws consciousness into crisis and, in multiple ways, brings the sufferer closer to a state of nonbeing in which her very humanity becomes questionable. Scarry's analysis of pain gives us the root understanding of how pain challenges a subject's humanity when she suggests that pain "obliterates" consciousness.[8] In addition to death, pain is one of "the most intense forms of negation, the purest expression of the anti-human, of annihilation, of total aversiveness."[9] It is the experience of pain, then, that can make a subject feel inhuman.

The remarkable legacy of black pain and vulnerability has been and continues to be an important element of American culture and African American identity. Nevertheless, the presence of pain and the specter of vulnerability have caused consternation in African Americanist critical discourse, especially in recent years when any semblance of sentimental rhetoric has been regarded with suspicion. The pathos of black subjectivity that prevailed in liberationist discourse before the civil rights movement gave way to the confrontational, masculinist discourse that characterized black power and other Afrocentrist movements by the late 1960s. As a consequence, we arrived at a retrospective assessment that bifurcates African American liberationist struggles in gendered terms, identifying as accommodationist, passive, and retrograde the invocation of black vulnerability whereas the reference to black power and virility is figured as active and progressive. However, as is often the case with such extraordinary binarisms, the strategies and realities of black liberation movements are far more nuanced and complex. As Malcolm X's oft-repeated aphorism exclaims, the free and protected articulation of black humanity has been undertaken "by any means necessary" and therefore recruited all the weapons in its arsenal, including the stealthy but potent power of the look.

Given this gendered casting of black liberation strategies, it should not be altogether surprising that the present study identifies women as bearers of some of the most significant visual gestures in the struggle for freedom and rights. From antilynching journalist Ida B. Wells to outraged mother turned activist Mamie Till to the unnamed enslaved cook whose deliberate fire demanded salvation from God or, as fate would have it, concerned neighbors, it has frequently been black women who have mobilized their keen understanding of the power of visual regard to improve substantially the circumstances for themselves and their racial kin. In this book, I seek to honor and acknowledge the humane insight of these women whose significant contributions to the cause cannot be written off as passive feminine gestures.

A slippery character, the look has been recruited to perform very specific work in the name of justice in the modern age by assembling a viewership that is moved to protest and eliminate the fatal racism endured by people of African descent in the United States. This book asks how looking and the notion of humanity have been woven into the history of black America. It examines the image of the African American body in pain and death because this history illustrates a narrative of humane insight that emerges at precisely the moment when the proof of the visible—what is called *positivism*—dominated liberal rhetoric.

Another, more recent thread in the history of modern black liberation movements is the troubling suspicion with which African American experiences of pain are viewed. According to Debra Walker King, the national appreciation of black pain has suffered from a situation in which "black people disappear while their bodies are constantly renewed as memorials to suffering" that harken back to the woundings of slavery and lynching.[10] This manifests in the present day with systematic denial of and restriction from pain-alleviating medications.[11] In other words, black pain is denied a reality in the present and yet it overdetermines an understanding of the black body in history. Despite these challenges, advocates for the recognition and protection of African American human rights have repeatedly turned to the visibility of the black body in order to advocate for change. Such scenes of black suffering face two challenges in the endeavor to move onlookers to action. On the one hand, pain and death are resolutely private experiences, locked tightly within the borders of an individual's fleshly body. On the other, blackness and racial difference recommended to some a radically different and intractable sensorial experience, one that does not process pain in the way that "normal" humans do. The struggle for articulating suffering, then, should be seen as a battle on two epistemological fronts involving language and race.

My discussion of pain focuses on its physical manifestation as sensation. Without disregarding the significance of the "mental and emotional wounding and trauma that threatens one's ability to move 'safely' into 'survival and wholeness,'"[12] I focus in this book on cataloging the work involved in translating physical sensation into a communicable discourse. Such translation work involves the approximations and transmutations that we understand to be the bedrock of language itself. Attending to how pain and even death are rendered discussable, this study reveals how black pain has been made to make sense.

To make pain legible to another is, of course, no simple task. King has contemplated the struggles and objectives of black experiences of pain, placing pain at the horizon of understanding that language seeks to broach.

> The only way this difference [between the sufferer and others] can be bridged is if pain becomes objectified. . . . [I]t must achieve recognition through strategies and signs that provide it with an oral or visual symbolic form. . . . It needs an interpretable signature . . . that moves individual expression . . . [toward] a world of language, image, and metaphor where the difficulty to understand becomes easily readable.[13]

Despite how irretrievably pain and death are cut off from language, they remain fundamental states of human existence and as such seek to be communicated. The physical reality or ontology of pain—what it is and how it feels to the sufferer—is distinct from the representation of pain—what it symbolizes and how it appears to the onlooker. The connection between these two modalities of pain—between experience and representation—is a negotiated and manipulated one. Indeed, death, and in particular violent death, reveals the obstacles and the stakes of making another body's condition legible and discussable for political work.

In looking at the dead or dying body, in person or in its photographic representation, there is no egalitarian reciprocity at play. In semiotic terms, the dead are not merely incapable of self-representation through language; rather, they are antithetical to language itself. To phrase this differently, it is not that the dead are beyond the capture of a self-constituting language, but that they are irredeemably cut off from language, forever unable to speak for themselves and about themselves. The images of dead and dying bodies, then, do not work on spectators by "speaking" back to them as some models of looking have suggested. Rather, they charge the spectator with the work of making sense; that is, in coming up with a language to account for both their inability to say what they mean (what is the point of my existence?) as well as for their final exit from the realm of meaning itself (what does my ceasing to exist mean for others?).

I am absolutely *not* considering these manipulations and utilizations of the black body in pain and death to be the consequence of black people's intuitive response to suffering and injustice. Quite to the contrary, I am insisting that these choreographies of humane insight are deliberate. Throughout the nation's history, African Americans often ingeniously understood the power of the image to effect radical change. This study takes up the sometimes imperfect but undoubtedly powerful attempts to make pain and its equally intractable partner, death, elicit humane insight and activate the protection of black humanity. This book does not argue that the visual display of black bodies in pain has been a universally effective and unproblematic solution to the devaluing and destruction of African American humanity. There have been and continue to be great costs involved in displaying black bodies in states of ruin. The greatest of these costs is of course the pain and death of those bodies whose images have been put to use by the liberation cause. Instead of unilaterally championing the spectacularizing of suffering and death, this study tracks the ways that the visual display of the body has been used by proponents of black freedom and dignity. It investigates the underlying beliefs that motivate that strategy and take black humanity to be a principle concern.

This book makes two major claims about looking and humanity. The first is that looking is an active gesture. My research into the lives and roles of the numerous witnesses, mourners, and mislabeled "bystanders" of racial violence has compelled me to rail against the long-standing opinion that looking is a passive and ineffectual endeavor. To the contrary, the actors in the episodes discussed—from Mamie Till who forced her eyes and then the eyes of the world to behold the destroyed body of her fourteen-year-old son, Emmett, to the many artists and gallerygoers who filed past graphic displays of lynching photographs to the former slaves and civil rights activists who exposed the abuse of their own bodies to an international media—all participated, actively, in the production and destruction of race and racism. Looking—either with humane insight or with its conspicuous absence—must therefore be understood as making an active contribution to our knowledge and experience of the world.

My second claim is that humanity is an ideological construct and, as such, neither its visual appearance nor its verbal testimony can confirm its presence in any absolute terms. I do take very seriously the long and frequently bloody battles of civil rights activists, past and present, who have put their lives on the line to ensure that all human beings are treated with the dignity they deserve. However, the concept of *humanity* functions quite distinctly in rhetoric. The term and the concept can only ever signal a truth that can be neither proven nor disproven. Humanity is therefore less of a condition than it is an idea that signals to others how those identified as human beings ought to be treated. And yet, this concept of humanity has been essentially contested territory for African Americans who have sought full recognition ensured by the moniker *human*; it is this quest that I designate with the movements identified as civil rights and black liberation. What I concede in this book is not that the movement is in vain, but that the terrain of contestation is not reality but rather the image. Civil rights and black liberation and the humanity that they aim to protect should be understood as a matter of perception. By this I do not mean or endorse a mercurial application of recognition of humanity; instead, I am advocating, in the spirit of ethics, a sustained practice of humane insight.

One of the conclusions that follows from these claims is that looking can be understood structurally and, consequently, as substantially disconnected from the racial identification of the onlooker. This study assesses multiple variables including the historical, cultural, and rhetorical environments in which visual encounters occur. Every look, like every utterance, is articulated by someone at a particular place and time. The body that looks and the environment in which that look takes place are imbricated in and determined by complex discourses of history, region, race, gender, and so on. But even if every looking gesture is singular, the networks of beliefs and cultural locations are nevertheless legible to us as discursive formations. In this study, then, I necessarily attend to the locations and context, broadly conceived, from where one looks, keeping in mind that race affects the discourse that makes sense of the look, not the look itself.

Acknowledging, then, that the visual encounter shapes the world in concrete ways, this book asks how looking and the notion of humanity have intervened in the history of black America. It argues against wholesale dismissals of "humanity" as a useful category for an ethical global society. This study is therefore in line with Paul Gilroy's proposition that liberalist dismissal of humanity as a useful concept is premature in its wholesale rejection of all universal concepts.[14] To imagine what Gilroy terms human beings' "elemental" vulnerability is to imagine humanity as an a priori reality with which we spectators must reckon. A notion of humanity, functioning ideologically, underwrites all representations of the black body, including—and especially—representations of the black body in distress. It follows that such a concern with ascertaining humanity via the image should be linked to a visual genre associated with proof and evidence.

Although claims of a racial hierarchy have since been largely rejected as unscientific and condemned as racist on the grounds of its unprovableness, important questions about the ontology of humanity nevertheless remain. When does humanity come into being? Who decides the terms by which we define humanity? And finally, what hope(s) can we invest in humanity? These questions arise from the discursive nature of our concept of humanity. Humanity does not simply identify a genus and species grouping, but indicates the natural expectations and protections that are always imagined to adhere to human bodies. The human body earns its symbolic power by its appearance in a network of rights discourse. Human rights operate as a credo, ideally agreed upon and protected by governing institutions charged with the welfare of its constituents. Even if human rights have not been materialized as civil rights, they continue to function as a credo and call to the bodies, organized and individual, who hold the value of their lives to a higher standard than that which is being articulated on the ground.

The focus on humanity here does not ignore the fact that, in the United States and other parts of the world, those identified as being of African descent have, often on the basis of the visual markers of race alone, been viewed and treated as outsiders to humanity. To view black people as human was often in the late eighteenth and nineteenth centuries a radical proposition that "called into question the rationales that legitimated the exclusion of blacks from the purview of universal rights and entitlements."[15] Pseudoscientific disciplines like phrenology, craniology, and anthropometry enabled racial taxonomies that ranked people of African descent at or near the bottom of the hierarchy of humankind. Curiously, though perhaps not surprisingly, the drive to exclude black peoples from the category of human coexisted alongside Enlightenment claims for universal equality and the rights of man.

A study of historical definitions of the ontology of the human reveal humanity to be a predominantly discursive phenomenon. The human has been an object of concern to human beings throughout history, and numerous contemplative traditions have sought to define it. As philosopher Emmanuel Eze has noted, modern societies' "beliefs about the varieties of humans" may only be understood by attending to philosophical ruminations on the essence of the human.[16] In their attempts to define the human, early religious and philosophical traditions look inside the body, to the soul and to consciousness. In these texts, the body is either a problem for or incidental to an understanding of the human.[17]

It is not until Friedrich Hegel's supplementation of consciousness with self-consciousness that humans are considered as fundamentally social beings whose knowledge of themselves depends upon being recognized by an Other. Hegel's dialectical relationship between the lord and the bondsman justifies as it describes inequity between two equally conscious beings. In the dialectic, the conscious being must encounter another conscious being in order to become aware of his uniqueness and the singularity of his particular consciousness; this is the necessary move toward self-consciousness. It is a relationship premised upon recognition—the recognition of the Self as a self by another Self. If we bear in mind how essential consciousness has become to the definition of the human, we see how the encounter with an Other's consciousness equates to the encounter with an Other's being and, subsequently, how recognition plays an essential role in the constitution of the human qua human. Nevertheless, Hegel's dialectic, which introduces intersubjectivity into the constitution of the Self and makes recognition by an Other an essential moment in man's struggle toward his self-realization, lacks a consideration of human bodies. It speaks only of an awareness of the Other's consciousness without indicating what sensual faculty—sight, touch, sound—prompts that awareness.

Other Enlightenment and pre-Enlightenment philosophers—namely Jean-Jacques Rousseau and Thomas Hobbes, respectively—discuss the human in society, but do not view the human's interaction with other humans as a defining condition. Rather, they view society as a secondary and even an artificial state that deforms and obscures the essential qualities of the human, preferring instead to contemplate *human nature.* And it is, I maintain, nature as a priori that has permitted minority and oppressed groups to be continually confronted with a hierarchy of being. As feminist philosopher Louise M. Antony points out, the term *man* that appears in the majority of these philosophers' tracts on the nature of man is not a linguistic accident but an assertion of their belief that *man's* nature—namely, his capacity for rational thought—is superior to *woman's*. The distinction these philosophers make between men and women in terms of their natures is subtle and convoluted, and the definition of *human nature* they propose is at continual risk of collapse. Antony reasons that the "solution to this problem . . . was to first affirm that women and men shared a nature but to then add the qualification that women were—by nature—unable to realize it fully."[18] This strategy permits women, and, I would argue, racial others, to be acknowledged as human beings while it preserves their perceived inferiority.[19]

The empiricist and scientific discourses of the eighteenth century onward, including—and especially—evolutionary theory, have made nature (often in competition with nurture) a primary concern and a ubiquitous term. Charles Darwin's theory of natural selection, which argues that those qualities best suited for survival are the ones that prevail, has reinforced the idea that nature knows best.[20] Furthermore, Darwin's insistence that nature is utterly objective in its privileging of certain biological aspects over others permanently silences any argument that an aspect (or even a species) that has been phased out has been rendered extinct unjustly. The problem for oppressed groups has lain in the application of Darwinism to modern social structures. One can easily see how those interested in arguing for the innate inferiority of women and nonwhites could transpose the "survival of the fittest" notion science associates with biological events to justify the social status quo.

Western human rights discourse is the most obvious inheritor of this long consideration of the ontology of the human. The ethical implications for a notion of humanity are the primary focus of human rights discourse—another field that depends upon defining (however cautiously) the human. The very concept of human rights is endorsed and protected (but not defined) by the United Nations' Universal Declaration of Human Rights that was established in 1948 in the wake of World War II and the revelations of the Holocaust. The idea that such a nebulous—and, I maintain, predominantly discursive—concept such as "the human" should prove foundational to a set of rights is a contentious issue for political theorists and philosophers.

The notion of humanity has proved a tendentious concept, particularly in the latter half of the twentieth century, when it was called upon to serve two masters—fascism and liberalism—and did so without favoritism. The purpose of humanitarian thinking, according to Nazi theorist Carl Schmitt, was to usefully differentiate those who were human from those who were not. For Schmitt, humanity was an essential component to the Nazi project of "imperialist expansion" and "economic imperialism" and was in line with the state's determination of worth.[21] Schmitt was, however, compelled to address the implicit universality and unavoidable benevolence of the term, confessing that

> [h]umanity as such cannot wage war because it has no enemy, at least not on this planet. . . . When a state fights its *political enemy* in the name of humanity, it is not a war for the sake of humanity, but a war wherein a particular state seeks to usurp a universal concept against its military opponent. At the expense of its opponent, it tries to identify itself with humanity in the same way as one can *misuse* peace, justice, progress, and civilization in order to claim these as one's own and to deny the same to the enemy.[22]

Some liberal theories that followed Schmitt's sought to restore human dignity to all persons. Ironically, these theories did so by embracing a similarly monolithic, a priori version of humanity that could not recognize difference.[23] As the recent work on capabilities studies by Martha Nussbaum and Amartya Sen shows, there is no guarantee that an individual's humanity (or as Nussbaum calls it, "human dignity") will be protected and recognized, although one may argue that is precisely what the work of a governing power should be.[24] Humanity is something that needs to be articulated and, most important, to be recognized.

What does it mean to recognize the human body in pain? One answer is that it means acknowledging the elemental, *pace* Gilroy, human condition of vulnerability.[25] This is vulnerability understood as a universality. Recognizing elemental vulnerability in an Other means recognizing the Other as human. The visual encounter is uniquely positioned to invite the spectator's interrogation of humanity. An investigation of how certain vulnerabilities are imaged and racialized can help explain how the recognition of a body as human can be regarded as a social and political act. The concept of humanity is useful and necessary to theories of social ethics and justice.

Appreciating the human body for its power to signify allows us to make sense of the black body's visual presence in struggles for the recognition and protection of black humanity. The degradation and suffering of the physical body indicates a violation of the basic human right to bodily integrity. The spectacle of black vulnerability draws upon the onlooker's investment in a shared humanity.

Racial identity has influenced not only the perception of pain and death but also the proximity to pain and death. This inequity forms the crux of Giorgio Agamben's reformulation of the Foucauldian concept of "bare life."[26] Selective vulnerability is the hallmark of exclusionary humanity such as that embraced by Schmitt. Under slavery, Jim Crow, and other insidious forms of systemic neglect, African American life has often been profoundly deformed by its backbreaking vulnerability and its tissue-thin proximity to death—a proximity that is not experienced so frequently or so devastatingly by those in power. The uncanny vulnerability of the black body has caused the establishment of economies based on black mortality. As Karla Holloway so deftly illustrates in her study of contemporary African American death culture, deaths of African Americans are often untimely and direct consequences of violence.[27] The particular contours of African American death can also be traced in the episodes of black vulnerability and black resistance chronicled in this current study.

People of African descent in the United States have succumbed to fatal acts of violence quite often and in great numbers. But on more than a few occasions, the sheer preponderance of visual evidence documenting that fact has motivated people to act or simply to think differently—to think and to act in accordance with a belief that black people are human beings. This book's preoccupation with the image, then, should be understood not as an interest in how the image represents truth or as a disinterest in actual bodies, but as an investment in how the kind of truth that the image can represent is ideologically encoded. In other words, I am advocating for a keener attention to what we might call *visual discourse* that foregrounds the relationship between the image and its spectator. We critics of visual culture must acknowledge that the beliefs that are held by the spectator largely end up determining how the image is interpreted and how the world is experienced. One of these beliefs—indeed, the one with which I am most invested here—is the belief in the existence of humanity. I am in some ways taking the image at face value: accepting that it can represent the humanity of human beings. This stance seems to me something that has been overlooked by theories of the image[28] that foreground mediation while either ignoring or downplaying the significance of humanity as a social signifier. We visual critics need a nuanced and flexible understanding of the image that can both acknowledge the technical aspects of photographic and other media and recognize the special work that the image does in the world, including supplying evidence of atrocities.

Looking at suffering does not only entail looking at its representation. Looking is also conducted "in the flesh" upon another's flesh, inhabiting the same space as the body being beheld. There are important distinctions to be made in the different kinds of looking this study includes, and this book acknowledges these in its attention to the mediation and contextualization of acts of looking. That said, this book does not take up the subject of the image in a conventional way. The objects of study that this work engages are not consigned to a unique medium, although photographic processes of reproduction do figure prominently in the discussion. What I seek to interrogate is the experience of visual encounter, a phenomenological experience that has intrigued numerous philosophers and theorists from disparate disciplines and that figures prominently in my consideration of what it means to encounter the existence of another human being through sight. Even as evolving visual technologies—such as photography, cinema, and digital imaging—recode our encounters with spectacular violence, they perpetuate the ethical injunction to bear witness. The nature and techniques of witnessing and of seeing have changed undeniably. But the basic mechanism for learning about humanity—the visual encounter with another being—remains. Though we may indeed inhabit a world no longer (if it ever was) characterized by our access to the actual but now by our encounter with the simulacrum, as ethical human beings, we continue to make recourse to an image of human respect and dignity—in a word, humanity—to justify and legitimize our living with others.

Organized chronologically, the following chapters trace the lineage of humane insight and spectacles of black pain and death in the past century and a half. They investigate incidents in African American visual culture that depend upon the recognition of humanity as an elemental component of human identity to be sought and secured. The image of the mortal, wounded, and dead black body grounds a politics of racial equity and justice in the language of pathos. Taken together, these visual episodes assert the importance of ethics and humanity in our analyses of race and visual culture.

The first chapter discusses the abolitionist movement and the rise of sensation as a rhetorical theme. By the end of the middle of the nineteenth century, we see a recognizably modern public entreaty for the image of the victim. According to literary critic Nancy Armstrong, the realist image was crucially reconfigured by the nineteenth century's positivist desires to obtain verification through the sense of sight and, later, by the satisfaction of those desires in the medium of photography. Following Armstrong's lead, this study understands the term *image* in its post-nineteenth-century sense as identifying both the *actual* ("this really happened") and the *conventional* ("this is what it looked like").[29]

Although photography was not in place during all of the moments under investigation in this chapter, the clamor for visual proof is consistently evident. The Lalaurie affair of 1834—a scandal in which a white Creole woman was found to have horribly experimented on her slaves for her own wanton pleasure—predicts the political utility of the view of the abused black body that will come to characterize black liberation practices into the twentieth century.

Whereas the first chapter considers the production of outrage produced by in-person spectacle and replicated in newspaper narratives, the second chapter investigates the recoding of images of lynchings that transformed the look itself from one of private pleasure to one of public disgust. Among these counter-looks—looks that endeavor to undo and even vilify the initial approving looks that lynching images invited—is the look of shame that operates as a kind of social policing mechanism, one that diminishes the possibility for the consumption of lynching imagery as pleasurable and entertaining. By comparing a recent exhibition of lynching photography with a mid-century exhibition of antilynching artwork, we see how different evaluative criteria—aesthetic, ideological, realist, documentary—suggest different political interpretations of lynching imagery. This chapter addresses directly the problem of how the images and the exhibitions work on the spectator as a social subject. In other words, the analysis here is invested in the visual regimes embedded in and authorized by the viewing environment.

The third chapter takes up the many visual encounters with the dead and disfigured body of Emmett Till (some in the flesh, some mediated by photography) to understand how the political ideas that would come to shape the civil rights movement in America were fomented and sometimes nearly thwarted. The decision of Mamie Till-Mobley (Emmett Till's mother) to have an open-casket funeral is at the heart of this chapter. Her radical gesture made possible the wide-scale circulation of photographs of Till's body. An examination of the courtroom in which Till's murderers were tried makes clear the paradoxical uses of his image. This use demonstrates that the political utility of seeing another's disfigured body lies in recognizing that the violence enacted upon the Other is also violence enacted upon the Self. Containing more theoretical approaches than any other section of the book, this chapter contains a psychoanalytic and deconstructionist examination of the recognition, which is figured as a central project in the struggle for black liberation and civil rights. The theoretical analyses that are here applied to the events involving Emmett Till are matched and balanced by the wisdom of Mamie Till-Mobley herself. Much of this chapter's project, therefore, entails catching up to and untangling the insights, humane and political, of a woman who understood keenly how looking works.

Till's murder and politicized funeral did, in fact, activate many of the interventions we now characterize as part of the civil rights movement. The fourth chapter addresses the publication of images depicting violence against people engaged in acts of nonviolent resistance. These acts, much like the look itself, are not to be considered passive in the proper sense, but are instead examined as deliberately choreographed dramatizations of injustice. The strategy of nonviolent direct action that was taken up during the freedom rides, lunch-counter integrations, and marches of the 1960s vividly demonstrated, often to a confounded mainstream press, the infringements upon black humanity and freedom of expression endured and indeed endorsed in the southern United States.

Although the images of police and mob brutality during the civil rights era now feature prominently in our visualization of national history, more recent images of black suffering have not been so positively assumed. Returning to New Orleans more than 170 years later when the city and the region suffered devastation in the wake of Hurricane Katrina, the final chapter considers the current state of the image of black suffering and death and questions whether the radical potential of humane insight continues.

This book unpacks and theorizes aspects of critical race spectatorship that are defined as visual encounters. In these encounters the viewer is called upon to identify explicitly his or her relationship to race and to (anti-)racism. The book focuses on events in which the look has been politically activated and mobilized for antiracist ends. These analyses call for nuanced appreciations of viewing relations, specifically as they mediate the experience of viewing black bodies in pain. To shift the critical gaze from the body or from the image to the idea of humanity as this book does is to make a subtle move with profoundly radical consequences for our understanding of the visual encounter.

1

Slavery's Suffering Brought to Light—New Orleans, 1834

On the morning of April 10, 1834, a fire broke out at the mansion on the corner of Royal and Governor Nicholls Streets in New Orleans's Vieux Carré. According to legend, the fire was started in the kitchen by an enslaved African American woman.[1] The house at 1140 Rue Royale belonged to Dr. Louis Lalaurie and his wife, Delphine Lalaurie, the latter the offspring of prominent white Creole parents and a fixture in New Orleans society. The arson was not an attempt at anonymous vengeance. The African American woman, who worked in the house as a cook, stayed to witness the consequence of her action. As she was chained to the kitchen floor, she had no other choice.[2]

Newspaper accounts and witness depositions explain that the fire precipitated a horrific discovery in the uppermost floor of the home. Rushing into the house, neighbors of the couple attempted to rescue the furniture from the flames (the cook, too, was taken to safety), but were thwarted from entering the locked upper chambers that the owners insisted contained nothing of importance. Those who ignored this claim and secured entry to the rooms were met by a startling scene in which, the local *New Orleans Bee* reports, "[s]even slaves, more or less horribly mutilated, were seen suspended by the neck, with their limbs apparently stretched and torn from one extremity to the other."[3]

The dreadful discovery was reproduced in vivid detail in newspapers throughout the country, including the *Essex Register* (Salem, Massachusetts), the *New Orleans Courier*, the *Louisiana Advertiser*, and New York's *Journal of Commerce*. Still more periodicals such as William Lloyd Garrison's

Boston-based abolitionist journal the *Liberator* and the national weekly publication *Niles' Register* reprinted the story in full.[4] The case was also published in the 1834 Philadelphia antislavery pamphlet *A Concise View of the Slavery of the People of Colour in the United States*.[5] It even met the eyes of a young Mary Todd Lincoln; as her niece Katherine Helm would later report, "Mary and [her cousin] Elizabeth shivered with horror over [the] revolting occurrence in New Orleans," and the subject remained on their minds and lips for days afterward.[6]

The news reports of the Lalaurie affair at the time solicited the emotional response of the Todds and all other readers, framing the event as revealing an untenable offense enacted upon enslaved black bodies. The newspaper narratives and other subsequent accounts, such as ghost stories and travelogues, indulged in the sensational telling of the crime, a telling that prominently featured graphic descriptions of the victims' injuries alongside detailed depictions of the presumably universal emotional response to the scene. The written descriptions depended upon the reader's imagination to inspire the emotional response—in a word, horror—that the accounts framed as appropriate. In so doing, the written accounts of the affair endeavored to replicate a moment of visual encounter. But in this, they could only ever fall just short of the goal, the description being structurally incapable of re-presenting the scene to a viewer. Elaine Scarry explains that this is due to the re-presentation being addressed to perception whereas presence is addressed to imagination. "[T]he imagined object," Scarry writes, "lacks the vitality and vivacity of the perceived one; it is in fact these attributes of vitality and vivacity that enable us to differentiate the actual world present to our senses from the one that we introduce through the exercise of the imagination."[7] The representational index—be it the word or the photographic image—can never satisfy to the same degree the quest for knowledge that presence—being in a place at the moment of the event or, I would add, sharing the space with the survivors of the event—can achieve.

Investigating the circulation and management of the Lalaurie case yields not only insight into the extremely complex and often contradictory ideas about the institution of slavery and humanity, but also the power accorded to sight at this historical moment as a means to acquire knowledge. The encounters, both in person and in print, with the suffering bodies of enslaved blacks and the humane insight of these confrontations challenged core principles of slavery and, at moments, exposed the cracks in slavery's logic that would eventually lead to its extinction. Through the smoke of the Lalaurie mansion, one perceives, albeit hazily, a view of black humanity.

The suffering of the enslaved black bodies who were rescued from the Lalaurie conflagration was described almost obsessively by contemporary newspapers, both abolitionist and mainstream. One local newspaper, the *New Orleans Bee,* offered a detailed description of the scene that was summarily reprinted in its entirety in the *Liberator.* The latter paper rallied for even more such exposures to be publicized for the sake of the abolitionist cause, declaring "we want much more. We wish persons who have resided long at the South, would publish still more of their observations. We wish to see pictures."[8] The *Liberator* was not alone in this desire. The syndicated publication of the Lalaurie story allowed readers nationwide to envision the terrible spectacle in New Orleans. The *Liberator*'s easy and eager repurposing of the mainstream *Bee*'s story for its own decidedly abolitionist purposes recommends an appreciation of the event for its foregrounding of one of the most convincing arguments and compelling evidence against the institution of slavery—namely, the vicious and unmotivated abuse of the enslaved. The article read as follows:

> The conflagration at the house occupied by the woman Lalaurie, in Hospital-street, has been the means of discovering one of those atrocities, the details of which seem to be too incredible for human belief. We would shrink from the task of detailing the painful circumstances connected therewith, were it not that a sense of duty, and the necessity of exposing and holding up to the public indignation, such a wretch as the perpetrator, renders it indispensable for us to do so. The flames having spread with alarming rapidity, and the horrible suspicion being entertained among the spectators, that some of the inmates of the premises were incarcerated therein, the doors were forced open for the purpose of liberating them. Previous, however, to taking this liberty, (if liberty it can be called,) several gentlemen, impelled by their feelings of humanity, demanded the keys, which were refused them, in a gross and insulting manner.[9]

The *Bee* hedges in its narration of events but not because it was ambivalent about the righteousness of Madame Lalaurie's violence.[10] Rather, the story qualifies its presentation of details by declaring its reluctance to indulge in its own depictions of gore. In effect, by declaring its reluctance, the story seeks to foreclose accusations that it enjoyed reporting unpleasantness. Lest the newspaper be accused of a sadism akin to that of Lalaurie, the report describes not only the scene but also its own revulsion at having to report on it.

Disqualifying interpretations of its reportage as a selfish and prurient act, the article reinscribes the report's publication as an act of duty. With this declaration of purpose, the *Bee* asserts the importance of witnessing terrible scenes and of giving a moral account of them. The vexation that the article performs pits the responsibility of looking upon a scene of bodily destruction against the horror and revulsion that is brought on by such visual encounters. The duty of looking, mimed in the prose and equated in the article with the duty of reporting, prevail in this case.

Mirroring the report's moral battle about the right to look is the related question of what looking can accomplish. The *Bee*'s prose configures the abuse of the enslaved as paradoxically both beyond human comprehension and needing to be seen. The paper bemoans its medium—the written word—for its inadequacy in offering "a proper conception of the horror." While written language is found wanting in its capacity to "inspire" horror, human imagination is praised for its capacity to reconstruct the scene in visual images in the mind's eye and "picture what it was."

The scene is depicted as not merely a visual event but an emotional one as well. Despite the putative impoverishment of the word, the article nevertheless uses words to provide a description of the scene. The resulting description eschews regarding the scene with an objective eye that would focus solely on the items and persons who are visually presented. Instead, it favors a look that is by default attached to the sensations of the onlooker. In so doing, the report privileges and implicitly advocates looking with humane insight as an appropriate if not preferable way to make sense of the event.

The article qualifies its looking with humane insight—a look that is, through the process of reading, mimed by its readers—as a painful but necessary project. The paper justifies the publication of this description as due to "the necessity of exposing [the abuse] and holding [it] up to the public indignation." This invocation of duty indicates the newspaper's underwriting ethos: that the publicizing of horrific events is a newspaper's compulsory response to atrocity. In essence, the publication of the story functions as a moral stopgap measure, defending against the danger that, should the event not be reported, it would succumb to the status of being "too incredible for human belief," and remain not just ignored, but denied as having ever occurred. The northern abolitionist publication the *Liberator* would later reflect upon this anomalous but, in its view, righteous exposure of slaveholding atrocity, observing that "[i]t is only when some case, like that of Lalaurie's, excites so much indignation, that the usual system of concealment is neglected, that the veil is raised for a moment, and we obtain a glimpse of the dreadful tragedies which it covers."[11]

Clamor for the firsthand view and for the knowledge that view could impart of course preceded the invention and circulation of documentary photographs. Other visual forms such as engravings could reproduce visual displays, but the word was frequently recruited to satisfy desires for the view as well. When firsthand witnessing was not feasible, linguistic representations like that featured in newspaper reports of the Lalaurie affair supplemented the desire for the visual display. Literary depictions of suffering such as those found in slave narratives and other firsthand accounts strove to bring the sight of black bodies before readers' eyes. Sally Gomaa contemplates such accounts in her examination of the 1839 compendium of suffering entitled *American Slavery As It Is: Testimony of a Thousand Witnesses* and Linda Brent's pseudonymous autobiography *Incidents in the Life of a Slave Girl* (1861). Gomaa explains that the "large scars" detailed in these books "provide a visual depiction of pain" and in fact "exemplify the visual requisites for sympathy in abolitionist discourse: a testimony without words."[12]

Such testimonies indicate the special authority granted to the body in general and to the suffering body in particular. Frederick Douglass is perhaps the most famous of the black authors to mobilize depictions of his bodily suffering to abolitionist ends. As one scholar contends, "Douglass's *Narrative [of the Life of Frederick Douglass]* marshals the visual power of the injured black body to convey the brutality of the South's peculiar institution."[13] For her part, historian Saidiya Hartman gives a judicious account of the reception of Douglass's representations of wounding that challenges any easy digestion of Douglass's sensational scenes. "Are we witnesses who confirm the truth of what happened in the face of the world-destroying capacities of pain . . . ?" Hartman asks, "Or are we voyeurs fascinated with and repelled by exhibitions of terror and sufferance?"[14] While there is no simple or definitive answer to these questions—each answer depends upon the reader and her circumstances—we can nevertheless examine the rhetorical standards and ideological standpoints that engender Douglass's explicit narrations of violence. Here, humane insight signifies a project of simultaneously accessing and recoiling from the depiction of pain. It seems clear, however, that the responsibility of reading with humane insight is laid at the feet of the present-day reader just as it was for Douglass's abolitionist counterparts.

As evinced by his autobiography as well as his speeches and letters, Douglass readily submitted his own body to the scrutinizing gaze of his readers. In a letter to one of his detractors, a fellow abolitionist named Samuel Hanson

Cox, Douglass invoked the woundings endured by his own body to prove his special knowledge of the antislavery cause. Directing his indignation at Cox's self-identification as an abolitionist, Douglass challenged that Cox's "great love of liberty, and sympathy for the downtrodden slave, ought to have led [him] to 'pardon something to the spirit of Liberty,' especially in one [such as Douglass himself] who had the scars of the slave-driver's whip on his back, and who, at this moment, has four sisters and one brother in slavery."[15] This description of his scar alongside mention of family members still held in bondage places Douglass squarely in a racial community characterized in the moment by physical and emotional pain. In the letter, his membership in the fraternity of black people wounded by slavery permits him "to represent three [million] of my brethren," with whom he "[had] been one . . . in their sorrow and suffering."[16] This reference to a community of black sufferers wounded under slavery's yoke is crucial to Douglass's rhetorical authority here. His reference to his own enduring (as opposed to momentary and past) pain is used to contradict Cox's dehistoricized description of Douglass as "petted, and flattered, and used, and paid by certain abolitionists."[17] Instead, Douglass presents a fully racialized and historicized body certain of the source of its own agency and authority. Rather than provide a "normalized representation of [black] suffering" that permits "black people [to] disappear while their bodies are constantly renewed as memorials to suffering," Douglass's prose works to reembody the abstract suffering of slavery through the description of his own wounded body.[18]

The representation of the slave body's wounds did not, in and of itself, constitute a radical refiguring of the black body. Just as actual bodies were exchanged, so too were their visual representations. The visual depictions of slaves "were repeatedly on view in woodcuts, lithographs, paintings and sculpture either as shackled, on their knees and begging for mercy or in desperate flight, footsore and with their belongings on their back," reinforcing the notion of the enslaved as powerless victims.[19] The image of the wounds, just like the image of the enslaved body, had to be interpreted in accordance with a sensationally informed concept of humanity in order to function as an antislavery appeal. An example of the abolitionist image of the disempowered black body is found in the 1787 Josiah Wedgwood–designed image of the kneeling slave that is accompanied by the query, "Am I not a man and a brother?" The image adorned many objects, including medallions and donation boxes, and implored its beholders to answer the question in the affirmative and to assess their understanding of kinship and humanity.

Lalaurie's victims did not, in fact, reap any substantial benefit from the recognition of their violation. Upon their rescue, they were housed in the public jail until they succumbed to death in the following days. During these final moments, they were viewed by a great number of New Orleans's free citizenry who sought to satisfy their fascination with the case by viewing with their own eyes the devastation wrought upon Lalaurie's former slaves. Consequently, many local readers did not have to leave the images of physical abuse to the scenes that the newspaper reports had inspired, but instead strode through the jailhouse to observe the actual bodies and actual wounds of the rescued. There was no shortage of onlookers. The April 12 edition of the *Bee* estimated that "[f]our thousand persons at least . . . have already visited these victims to convince themselves of their suffering."[20] As long as the slaves remained alive, an audience was ensured.

Yet it was not only African American bodies that were on display at the jail. Late nineteenth-century author Henry Castellanos records that "[n]umberless instruments of torture, not the least noticeable of which were iron collars, 'carcans,' with sharp cutting edges, were spread out upon a long deal table, as evidences of guilt."[21] Arguably, the weapons indicated more than just the Lalauries' guilt. They also contributed to onlookers' assessment of the slaves' wounds and a further enhancement of their perhaps unwitting appreciation of those bodies' pain. The suffering of the black body as well as instruments of pain were the objects of the spectators' visual inquiry.

In this jailhouse encounter, visitors were called upon not only to witness the effects of Delphine Lalaurie's violence but also to condemn that violence as sadism. But the caliber of that sadism was measurable not in the tools of torture but in the wounds on the body—on *black* bodies, specifically. The looking arrangement that was staged in the jailhouse—an arrangement that mirrored the one that faced the neighborly rescuers—was necessarily inflected by the recognition of white depravity *and* black vulnerability. Consequently, the jailhouse viewers who beheld the dying bodies of Lalaurie's former slaves were invited to imagine for a moment the experience of black pain.

Indeed, the Lalaurie scandal epitomizes a key moment when black pain could be recognized as an unwarranted and untenable experience. It is worth pointing out that the dominant narrative of the event—one that emerged mere hours after the initial fire and continued to hold in the many instances of its retelling—vilified Madame Lalaurie and cast the wounded black inmates as incontrovertible victims. We should interpret this narrative as supplying an important index of acceptable public discourse in the local free populous and note especially that this discourse provides space for the acknowledgment of black suffering. Discursive recognitions of black pain such as these allowed abolitionist discourse, and black liberationist discourse in general, to take the next step in recruiting the black body's experience of pain to testify for black humanity.

Discussions of and responses to the Lalaurie affair and to other illustrations of the pain of the black enslaved were deeply embedded in the sensational humanitarianism that was on the rise as abolitionist sentiment gained wider appeal. The demand for empirical evidence that characterizes humanitarian logic emerged, as historian Barbara Shapiro demonstrates, in the seventeenth century and transcended multiple disciplines—namely religion, history, law, literature, and the natural sciences.[22] By the middle of the nineteenth century, humanity was conceived as presentable to an observer—perhaps not without the aid of aesthetic cues, but communicable nonetheless. Addressing the technique of using sentimental narrative, historian Thomas Laqueur has argued that compassion for one's fellow man was at the heart of eighteenth- and early nineteenth-century humanitarian thought and that this conception of compassion found its natural way into literary production. According to Laqueur, the "aesthetic enterprise" that he identifies as the "humanitarian narrative is characterized in the first place by its reliance on detail as the sign of truth."[23]

Knowledge in the late eighteenth and nineteenth centuries increasingly came to be understood through the rubric of empiricism that privileged embodied experience and sensation rather than pure reasoning and contemplation as the truest routes to understanding the world. Sentimentalism, which can be understood as an attention to and highlighting of embodied sensations such as pleasure and pain, came then to inform both scientific and spiritual inquiries into the nature of humanity and dictated in both America and Britain what one scholar has called "the culture of sensibility" that encouraged "humanitarian feeling" and compassion.[24] Sentimentalism rose to dominate the discourses of pain during the late eighteenth and early nineteenth centuries through an enlightened Protestant, and especially late eighteenth-century Quaker, moralism that condemned cruelty and introduced the concepts of "*humaneness, sympathy,* [and] *benevolence.*"[25] Yet this morality of pain and cruelty—also called *sentimentality*—neither automatically nor necessarily bolstered the belief that black bodies experienced pain as "civilized" and implicitly white bodies did.[26]

The witnessing of another's suffering was by turns perceived as crucial to the elicitation of proper moral feeling on the one hand and as a reprehensible indulgence in cruelty on the other. In her essay on the rise of humanitarianism and pain in the American and British contexts in the eighteenth and nineteenth centuries, Karen Halttunen observes the prevalent ideal of "spectatorial sympathy," which would "teach virtue by softening the heart and eliciting tears of tender sympathy," thus impressing upon the spectator a properly sentimental morality.[27] However, Halttunen remarks, this "spectatorial sympathy" was also vehemently condemned by those who perceived the sentimental encounter to be a form of sadism characterized by self-indulgence and voyeurism.[28] Sentimentalism did not guarantee what acts could be designated as cruel; instead, it enforced the modern idea that suffering was not humankind's lot and that pain and cruelty were avoidable.[29] Consequently, proslavery advocates designated emancipation as a form of cruelty that would release former slaves into a dangerous world for which they were ill-equipped.[30]

Sentimentalism was not only used to glorify the benevolence of slavery. Sentimentalism was also put into service by pseudoscientists and proslavery advocates to prove the inferiority of certain racial groups deemed to be insensate or to have underdeveloped sensations. Paired with theories of inheritance and polygenesis, such notions were circulated by proponents such as the infamous zoologist Louis Agassiz in their self-serving racial mapping of the world. Fifteen years after mechanical photographic reproduction was made possible in 1835, Agassiz exploited the new tool of the era—the daguerreotype—to "supplement his anthropometric evidence with visible proof of 'natural' difference in size of limbs and configuration of muscles, establishing once and for all that blacks and whites did not derive 'from a common center.'"[31] The images he commissioned photographer J. T. Zealy to produce fall neatly within the genre that Allan Sekula has identified as "*instrumental realism*": a "representational project devoted to new technologies of social diagnosis and control, to the systematic naming, categorization, and isolation of an otherness thought to be determined by biology and manifested through the 'language' of the body itself."[32] Agassiz's putatively scientific aims, however, were predetermined, and the images he had produced were figured as guarantees of a preexisting knowledge of the black body's elemental inferiority. The images' function for Agassiz as sufficient proof of distinct, multiple racial origins is prefigured in an earlier correspondence, one that predates the actual images. In a letter to his mother dated December 1846, Agassiz reacted to his encounter with the black domestics in his hotel, writing that "the feeling they inspired in me is contrary to all our ideas about the confraternity of the human type and the unique origin of our species."[33]

Agassiz's strategy of presenting his own abiding belief in "the confraternity of the human type" as being overthrown by the empirical "data" supplied by the hotel domestics is a remarkable rhetorical move in that it puts the onus of being excluded from humankind on the black person's body rather than on Agassiz's own (metaphorical) shoulders.

Such problematic investments in radically distinct racial sensibilities hinged imperialism and dominance to civilization and human advancement. Recently, scholar Kyla Schuller has explained how this mid-nineteenth-century organization of eugenicist thinkers understood sentiment to be an issue of race and intellectual advancement. In the opinion of these thinkers, "Sentiment ensures that the actions of the civilized are directed toward a larger social good, rather than toward private pleasure. . . . [Paleontologist Edward Drinker] Cope and his cohort posited that racial progress stems from the ability of the civilized to control the impulses of their body through the faculty of sentiment."[34] With respect to this postulate, the question arises as to how sensation was to be evaluated. For Cope and his colleagues, the measure was the body's display "in which the fineness of physical tissue correspond[ed] to delicacy of emotional feeling."[35] The visible indexes of the body's sensations were offered as empirical proof, but this offering of evidence, mystified by the mantle of science, neglected and endeavored to conceal the subjective mediation integral to the rendering of another's bodily sensations as proof. It does not take much probing to reach the question that troubles the logic of sentimental empiricism: Outside of language, how does the body articulate sensation?

When undergoing painful conditions, the body can deceive its onlookers—a point that is explored studiously in Saidiya Hartman's discussion of the forced performances of enslaved black bodies in antebellum America. Hartman refers to these forced performances of pleasure—the demand placed upon bodies at auction to "step it up lively"—as moments of disavowal that maintained a logical division between the enslaved black body's underdeveloped and uncivilized sensation ("No, the slave is not in pain. Pain isn't really pain for the enslaved, because of their limited sentience.") and the free white body's sophisticated and superior sensibility ("[T]he slave is happy and, in fact, his happiness exceeds 'our' own.").[36]

As powerful as sentiment and sensation were to those who would seek to define humanity through the experience of pleasure and pain, the private nature of those sensations stymied any attempt to define the human absolutely. The resistance of pain to intelligible expression, a feature documented so well by Scarry and Hartman, was a daunting aspect to any who sought in the name of pain to eliminate human suffering. That impasse was breeched by the sentimental onlooker's imagination. That look precipitated an imagined access to the sufferer's interior self, a self that knew but could not transmit its own very private experience of pain.

The melding of sensationalist rhetoric and positivist thought turned all bodies into important sites of knowledge and of moral virtue. With the body figured as a site of knowledge, awaiting discernment by an educated moral interpreter, in abolitionist campaigns the black body was looked to as providing the truth of its own humanity. The privileged sentimentalism of the abolitionist movement highlighted the political potential of the look. Looking upon such bodies with humane insight and imagining its internal human experience of pain was crucial to the efficacy of the abolitionist cause. Humane insight was not only an empathic gesture affecting the individual but a political gesture as well, one that influenced social politics and engendered change in the real world.

Antislavery advocates advertised this body-truth by recruiting the image of the black body to reveal its pain and to thereby illustrate the evils of slavery. The sight of the wounded black body proved more powerful even than verbal descriptions and testimonies of slavery's injustice. As we know from the photographs and drawings circulated by abolitionists (the photograph known as "The Scourged Back" is perhaps the most famous of these), the wounded body of the enslaved was a key image in the fight to end slavery. Consequently, "abolitionists' use of the slave's scarred body was shaped by the cultural and historical factors that were [by the mid-nineteenth century] beginning to sentimentalize pain."[37] The wounded body signified in distinctly powerful ways during the nineteenth century as a result of the rise of sentimentalism and a new appreciation of pain as an avoidable experience. Pain and its partner, cruelty, came under moral scrutiny and were acknowledged for the ways they deformed what was deemed to be the proper human experience.

The rhetoric of the abolitionist movement held other, nonenslaved bodies to be enduringly wounded as well. For many white abolitionists who had not suffered enslavement themselves, the physical deformation of the enslaved body through whippings, brandings, shootings, and amputations indicated not so much the pain of the black sufferer's body but the deformation of a sympathetic white Christian morality. A self-styled "friend" of the *Liberator* declared himself in that paper to be "sick at the inhumanity of the people" in Boston who would not rise to the cause of the immediate cessation of slavery.[38] Lamenting that "[a]rguments are wasted upon" such people, the writer suggests that an incapacity to reason is a quality that characterizes inhumanity.[39] Such depravity, according to the author, is an affliction that he provocatively proposes to correct through a sensorial experience—his own application of the lash to the "naked skin" of the humanely insensate—that would produce, he predicts, "convincing proof that [bondage] is not altogether so pleasant as they seem to imagine it to be."[40] The editor of the column adds another deficiency that, in his view, marks the inhumane—a spiritual barrenness. The editor adds that he was, therefore, "glad to learn that a great revival of religion is going on among them; for it is evident there is the utmost need of it. May it teach them to love their neighbor as themselves, and to do as they would be done by."[41] Such core losses of humanity as that described in this letter register as a lack of virtue that troubles dominant society's vision of its own humanity.

Another anonymous writer to the press understands the loss of compassion as an indication of an impoverished national character. The writer who describes him- or herself again as a friend to the publication as well as to "les noirs" praises the periodical for its "recording of such instances of cruelty to negro slaves."[42] The writer then submits his or her own examples, explaining that she or he saw "no other way in which a citizen of the free states can wash his hands of this national guilt, and stand justified to his conscience and his God, but by using his influence to remove and prevent" these cruelties.[43]

There was a significant drive among both black and white antislavery advocates to make the wounds of slavery more accessible to a public in need of a sensorial understanding of slavery's ills. Bearing witness in the flesh was the preferred method, so much so that an antislavery meeting held in Lynn, Massachusetts, in 1844 passed a resolution inviting "our lacerated brother . . . to travel through the northern States, expose his scars to the public gaze, and tell the story of his wrongs and sufferings to thronged assemblies of the people."[44] At abolitionist meetings, former slaves obliged to discuss and display the wounds that their bodies bore. In 1855, at the New England Anti-Slavery Convention, a former slave named Anthony Burns, "a living, breathing, moving witness of the great iniquity of slavery," indulged the assembled audience by "show[ing] the scars on his wrists [that resulted from] the irons he wore for four months in Virginia."[45] The abolitionist stage allowed for the coupling of the spectacular wound and the testimony of the speaker to transform the black body "from 'thing' to 'man.'"[46]

The invocation of black humanity did not, however, necessarily indicate a universalist understanding of humanity or the acceptance of African Americans as fellow human beings. Humanity had of course been recruited to very different ends in the early avocation of slavery as a significant part of a global Christianizing mission. That project could conceive of different levels of humanity that corresponded to a subject's relative achievements on a properly Christian path. In the absence of any absolutist determinations and subject only to self-serving divine interpretations, black humanity could be partitioned as a distinct condition, one that understood African heritage to signify a special fitness for servitude and submission. Under this system, black humanity suffers under an exclusionist sovereign regime that compels black human beings to lead what Georgio Agamben has called a "bare life."[47] As this selective humanity brings African Americans into greater proximity with suffering and death, it brings into focus the racism of the state. In the institution of American slavery, the state rendered black pain not only preferable, but profitable.

But even the laws of nineteenth-century American slavery placed a nominal limit on the infliction of black pain. In essence, if the pain did not bring about profit—that is, if the infliction of pain upon the enslaved was not done to bring about better work but merely to provide valueless personal entertainment—the law could be called upon to bring the account back into balance. It is through this logic that the New Orleans newspaper referred to Lalaurie's black victims as "seven of the *declared* heirs of 'inalienable rights' upon earth."[48] With their bodies cast as profitable bodies and by premising black humanity on financial rather than spiritual terms, the enslaved could also be identified as rights-bearing bodies that in principle had legal recourse to the violence they endured. In New Orleans, the humanity of Lalaurie's victims was only indicated insofar as their bodies were rights-bearing bodies. The enslaved victims of Madame Lalaurie were figured as protectable through the slave laws of the parish.[49] In these laws, colloquially referred to as "black codes" or "slave codes," the enslaved were recognized as possessing a qualified human status that revealed vividly slavery's commitment to different classifications of humankind.

Well before the fire, in fact, the law had been invoked to censure the Lalauries and to prohibit the violence enacted upon those they held as slaves. By the time of their ultimate exposure in 1834, the Lalauries had long been suspected by neighbors of abusing their slaves. Delphine Lalaurie's social guests and neighbors observed and reported "that several of her slaves appeared to be undernourished."[50] As a result, "an American lawyer sent a young Creole associate to advise Madame concerning the legal complications that one could experience for foul treatment of slaves."[51] The law was not permitted to intervene, however, as the lawyer "concluded that the rumors were without foundation."[52] Had she been drawn up on a crime, Lalaurie would have been accused of violating Louisiana's civil code on slavery that was set into law in 1825. In particular, she would have been found in violation of article 173, chapter 3, which states that "[t]he slave is entirely subject to the will of his master who may correct and chastise him, though not with unusual rigor, nor so as to maim or mutilate him, or to expose him to the danger of loss of life, or to cause his death."[53]

Codes such as this granted the slave some small legal recourse to the protection of his bodily integrity, but in practice this law was rarely enforced. The infamous codes were established to codify and to some extent justify rationales for slavery that were increasingly being viewed as untenable and illogical. Abolitionist William Goodell, who collected and published a compendium of these codes in 1853, concluded that all the legal precedents that existed to validate the enslavement of another human being were in staunch opposition to the national principle of individual human rights. Insofar as the black codes provided a mode of legal recourse for those enslaved, Goodell countered, "What protection *can* [the black codes] bestow so long as, by sustaining or even permitting or tolerating human chattelhood, *or failing to suppress it as a crime,* they leave not the slave the possession of one single right of humanity *to be* protected?"[54] Goodell's question reveals the selective use of humanity in the legalization of slavery. Rejecting the notion of selective humanity, Goodell indicts the law for its biased application of the concept.

Goodell's tract takes on deeply held and deeply conflicted philosophical and national principles about the rights of man. In his prose, the institutionalization of human bondage is presented as legally indefensible in the humanist, democratic society that the United States envisioned itself to be. His straightforward designation of the enslaved as human beings leaves no room for the sentimental hedging that would align the enslaved black person's experience of pain as more like that of animals than of human beings. Goodell's assertion of black humanity, echoed by abolitionists throughout the country and the world, is an instance in which the notion of universal humanity is called upon to defeat an exclusionary, mercenary, and ultimately racist wielding of humanity that protects some human bodies while it exposes others to vulnerability, pain, and death.

In the absence of any legal suit, some outraged free citizens of New Orleans took it upon themselves to exact a price from the Lalauries for their depravity. The scandal moved many onlookers to mount a riot against the Lalaurie edifice at 1140 Royal Street. The riot was the city's first ever.[55] The makeup of the crowd is contested, although white New Orleans writer George Washington

Cable reported in the *New Orleans Courier* that "[t]hose who rush in are of all classes and *colors,*" a detail contradicted by "a survivor of to-day who was there and took part."[56] All present were united in their aim to destroy the now-vacant building, and their success in this endeavor was substantial. In a letter from a New Orleans local that appears in a northern paper, five thousand people were reported to have assembled the night after the discovery.[57] The *New Orleans Bee* estimated that the damages to the Lalaurie home and furnishings amounted to $40,000; other reports claim figures closer to "11 to $13,000."[58]

The quantifying and monetizing of the destruction is provocative when one considers this destruction of property to have been inspired, in the eyes of the law, by another destruction of property—the Lalauries' unwarranted abuse of their slaves. We can see in the rioters' action and their choice of target—the Lalauries' residence—a rejection of article 462 of the state's 1825 civil code that, per article 455, defines slaves as "immovables" akin to "[l]ands and buildings, or other constructions . . . [that] are immovable by their nature."[59] Although the code itself announces a flawed logic by admitting that "[s]laves, though movables by their nature, are considered as immovables, by the operation of law," the application of law effected a reality in which enslaved persons "were bound by the same rules governing any transfer of real estate in the state."[60] Despite this legal definition, the riot enacted a radical distinction between enslaved beings and immovable property.

The vengeful crowd that assembled before the Lalauries' vacated home and the subsequent riot that entailed point to vexed perceptions of the black slave body in legal and economic terms. The distinction between inanimate property and human property made by the rioters is evident in contemporary newspapers' qualified censoring of the riot that hedged,

> although the provocation pleads much in favor of the excesses committed, yet we dread the precedent. To say the least, it may be excused, but can't be justified. Summary justice [such as that enacted upon the Lalauries' house], the result of popular excitement in a government of laws, can never admit of justification, lest the circumstances be ever so aggravating.[61]

This condemnation of what essentially amounts to mob justice is remarkable precisely because of its qualifications; that is, the article forbids this execution of unauthorized justice and endorses the protection of the Lalauries' house on the bases of law and decorum alone.

As radical as this distinction is in its de facto flouting of slave law, the protest cannot be said to indicate an incontrovertible honoring of the enslaved's *human* rights. As James Turner offers in his genealogy of modern attitudes toward animals and humanity, the mid-nineteenth century was a period during which the status of animals as rights-bearing beings was vigorously debated on both sides of the Atlantic.[62] Discussions about the humane treatment of animals retained an entrenched investment in hierarchy, with the Society for the Prevention of Cruelty to Animals "envision[ing] kindness slowly trickling down to the lower orders from their increasingly *humane* superiors."[63] Agitating on behalf of the disempowered indicated more about the humanity of the protestor than about the humanity of he who was being defended. If the rioters were indeed acting on behalf of the enslaved as retribution for their suffering instead of the more likely event that they were aiming to punish Lalaurie for her cruelty and inhumanity, their perception of the enslaved's suffering did not necessarily indicate a recognition of their full humanity.

The riot is therefore a far cry from the radical ideological intervention into the concept of black humanity that would ideally underwrite a protest against racialized violence. Though faulty in its premise and incomplete in its success, the riot does nevertheless indicate an appreciation of sentience—specifically the unnecessary experience of pain—and of pain itself as actionable occurrences. Moreover, the particular action taken by the rioters—to destroy Lalaurie's inanimate property as payback for her destruction of "human property"—is noteworthy in its subtle undermining of the objectifying logic of slave law. By identifying their destruction of property as an act of justice altogether distinct from Lalaurie's destruction of "property," the rioters refused, perhaps unconsciously, to equate Delphine Lalaurie's desecration of "her" black bodies (as the paradoxical logic of slavery held it) with their desecration of the edifice and furnishings.

It is disheartening but probably not surprising that the pain of black bodies whose suffering was caused by the peculiar institution of slavery and the codified nonexistence of black humanity under that regime effected little care for the well-being of those bodies. Newspaper reports of their existence disappear after the horrifying discovery. Their names are lost to history, the consequence of the free public's lack of care for anything more than their bodies' distress. Yet it is worth imagining that care for their lives was there and that it was profoundly expressed by a figure who, according to culture and law, possessed no humanity of her own with which to enact humane insight.

"Without being superstitious," an article in the *New Orleans Bee* notes, "we cannot but regard the manner in which these atrocities have been brought to light as an especial interposition of heaven."[64] But the fire was most likely not an act of God or a feature of fate. As several accounts suggest, the fire may well have been a deliberate act of sabotage enacted by the enslaved black female cook. Considering the fire as an intentional act compels us to address the presence of African American female agency and its effective intervention in a scenario of intolerable racial cruelty. Despite being cast by slavery as incapable of action and then further immobilized with chains attached to the kitchen floor, the black woman who the Lalauries held as an enslaved cook was able to exercise compassion and to seek protection of her and her fellows' corporeal dignity. Though we cannot know for sure as she, too, has been lost through the disregard of history, it is thrilling to think of this woman as viewing herself and the others who were enslaved by the Lalauries with humane insight. In herself and in her fellows, she saw human beings who did not deserve suffering but who were worthy of protection.

2

Framed and Shamed

Looking at the Lynched Body

After slavery, lynching became the next spectacular threat against African American bodies. With the abolition of slavery codified by the Emancipation Proclamation of 1863 and ratified by the Thirteenth Amendment to the US Constitution in 1865, large numbers of African Americans could legally possess their own bodies and publicly express their humanity in ways that had been foreclosed to them since Africans were first brought to the fledgling colonies as slaves.[1] In law, at least, blacks could now claim the civil rights guaranteed to all American citizens and protected by the country's instruments of law. But the special proximity to pain and death that black people endured during enslavement was not alleviated by the passage of laws that nominally recognized them as human. The driver's whip and the master's hand gave way to the mob's rope and fire. Once again, this time with lynchings, black pain and death were brought dramatically into view.

Lynching spectacularizes the threat to African American bodies in order to concretize a racial hierarchy in which whites are the arbiters of justice and keepers of humanity while blacks suffer under the shadow of death, a fate from which the law provides no relief. Lynching makes the visibility of the black body a requirement of its project of racial oppression. The lynched body is fundamentally a visible body, a body that is born of the spectacle of lynching itself. Yet, as with the antislavery movement, the antilynching movement also used the imagery of black suffering to foment nationwide, multiracial outrage.

All viewers of lynching images, regardless of historical location, national and regional affiliations, and even racial identification, encounter the battle for humanity that is depicted in the lynching scenario and documented and circulated in lynching photographs. In the lynching event and in its representations, racial entitlements and humanity are on display. The definitions and assignations of each are challenged and rewritten with every look that is laid upon them. The curated exhibitions of lynching images in the mid-twentieth century and early twenty-first century have endeavored precisely to contain the instability of the look by fomenting looking relations that seek to guarantee appropriate outrage and humane insight. This chapter examines the aesthetics of exhibition in two antilynching shows—the 1935 *Art Commentary on Lynching* mounted by the National Association for the Advancement of Colored People (NAACP) and James Allen's 2000 traveling exhibition *Without Sanctuary.*

As an image, the lynched body is a site of contested meaning. The image of the lynched subject is, according to Leigh Raiford, "a site of threefold struggle over the meaning, possession, representation, and memorialization of the black body."[2] In addition to Raiford, historian Amy Wood has thoroughly and thoughtfully accounted for the important transcoding of lynching images—from objects of terrorism to evidence of abuse—in her study *Lynching and Spectacle* (2009). Their work and that of many others, including Koritha Mitchell's *Living with Lynching* (2011) and Jacqueline Goldsby's *A Spectacular Secret* (2006), have enabled us to better appreciate the racial, regional, and cultural impact of lynching and the centrality of ritualized performance and public visibility involved in lynchings.[3]

These works and many more have expanded our understanding of lynching as a historical event fundamentally informed by the dynamics of visual and performance aesthetics. The scholarship on the antilynching campaigns and their recoding of lynching photographs and logic is also quite vast and usefully complicates our appreciation of the politics of violent imagery. This chapter does not seek to replicate that work, but instead to offer a phenomenology of the antilynching visual encounter—an encounter that deliberately calls upon the viewer's understanding of humanity—through an analysis of the visual curation at play in antilynching gallery exhibitions. To facilitate that project, however, a précis of key insights into the logics of lynching and the antilynching movement are worth reciting here.

Lynching has come to be understood primarily as a system of racial terrorism. Philip Dray, in his monumental study of lynching, explains lynching's familiar terms.

> By . . . 1905, lynching had come almost exclusively to mean the summary execution of Southern black men.

> Lynchings, even where they have been the accepted norm, have always disturbed many Americans. This is not simply because they are barbaric, inhumane acts, but because they inherently disavow a right Americans hold dear—the right to due process before the law.[4]

What Dray describes here is precisely a worldview of the empowered white and the disempowered black (man). But even as this worldview is one that lynching supposedly enacts and secures, it is one that is also always "disturbing" to the social fabric. Lynching attempts to cover up the anxieties over its righteousness with a spectacular display that is passed off as certainty. It ritualizes and performs white racial dominance and elicits black vulnerability and submission. The lynchings that occurred throughout the United States but especially in the South during the first half of the twentieth century "enacted and embodied the core beliefs of white supremacist ideology, [by] creating public displays of bestial black men in visible contrasts to strong and commanding white men."[5] Not only black men but also black women were configured as less than human beasts well before the lynchings that sought to secure that designation.

In addition to counteracting the humanity of black victims, lynching also consolidated white identity as righteous and just, a community of truly human beings who protect the region's social and species order. The enactment of white solidarity that was essential to the persistence of a way of life, often characterized as white men protecting white women from black men, was conducted over the body of the black lynching victim and performed in the lynching ritual. That spectacle functioned to affirm the strength of white dominance and enforce black submission.

Lynching was a ritual that was deliberately used by whites, predominantly in the Deep South, to distance their humanity, understood in large part to mean their exceptional subjectivity as rights-bearing citizens, from a black population that did not merit the protections afforded by the declaration of universal humanism of the nation's founding documents. The claims of the Declaration of Independence and its linking of American citizenship with universal humanity were an important touchstone for those agitating against lynching. Both the national and the universal principles articulated the sanctity of the body and defended the human right to embodiment. Denying African Americans jurisprudence and regulated punishment and instead releasing them to a doomed fate in the lynching spectacle meant refusing to recognize black bodies as rights-bearing citizens who were owed the due process that, in principle, the Declaration of Independence—in its democratic application of habeas corpus—upheld. The application of the rights of man expressed in the founding national document to African Americans registered among prolynching constituents as anathema, upholding the logic that "the legal system bestowed too many rights on black criminals and too little respect for white victims."[6] The lynching of African Americans reinforced the notion of the inhuman black subject by casting blacks as noncitizens, undeserving of rights and unrecognizable to the law.

The white dominance that found itself in crisis after the emancipation of black slaves demanded renewed spectacles of the black body's inhumanity. Lynching and its partner Jim Crow worked strenuously to obliterate the possibility of a humane insight that could be directed toward blacks. In lynching, the obliteration of humane insight was sought through the obliteration of its object—the black body itself. The display of the dead, tortured black body in the flesh and in the photograph, illustrating to all who saw its violent eviction from the community of living beings, constituted a basic convention of lynching that was originally meant to signify the ejection of the inhuman from the world of the living.

The broken black body was lynching's most potent symbol of racial subjugation. Lynch mobs used not only the dramatic stagecraft of the lynching event but also photographs, frequently circulated as postcards, to illustrate white dominance and black submission. Photographic postcards of lynching ensured that absentees could nevertheless participate in a crucial part of lynching—the spectacle—by looking at its representation. As Shawn Michelle Smith explains, the postcard's "circulation maps an imagined community of senders and receivers who share feelings for one another and, perhaps, for the scenes the postcard represents," adding that, in one photographic postcard in particular, "[t]he gap of space and time that separates [the] white mother [who received the card] and son [who sent it] will be sutured over the dead body of an African American man; sentimental white familial bonds will be reinforced through black death."[7] This virtual community of exceptional whites, like the mother-son bond Smith describes, is shored up over the dead body of its abject Other—the deceased black subject who is recognized as having no claims to the rights, justice, and humanity that is the proper domain of whites. The lynched black body signifies the racial abyss between whites and blacks as it bridges disparate bands of whites.

Just as abolitionists recruited spectacles of black pain and mortality to denounce slavery, the antilynching campaigns mobilized images of black suffering to illustrate the injustice of lynching. Nonetheless, a crucial distinction separates the antilynching movement's displays of lynching's black victims from the previous movement's displays of slavery's victims. Although arguing for black humanity was essential to both movements, the antilynching campaign had to contend with an opponent that had effectively incorporated images of lynching victims to serve its white supremacist agenda. Whereas the antislavery movement made much of exposing the heretofore hidden and disguised suffering of African Americans, the antilynching movement faced a foe that utilized the spectacle of black suffering as part of its campaign of racial terrorism. If the antilynching movement was compelled to make the image of the black body in pain operate in service to its cause—the outlawing of lynching—it needed first to make the lynched black body signify not the inevitability of its inferiority and oppression but the untenable violation of black personhood.

The ambiguity of the image was fully exploited by the antilynching movement. Employing tactics of visual recoding developed by activist Ida B. Wells and replicated by the NAACP, the antilynching movement capitalized on the disturbance that is arguably at the heart of lynching. Wells's 1895 pamphlet, *A Red Record: Tabulated Statistics and Alleged Causes of Lynchings in the United States, 1892–1893–1894,* featured a photograph of a lynching alongside the names, dates, and locations of the lynchings she had recorded during the three-year period. In *A Red Record, Southern Horrors: Lynch Law in All Its Phases,* and other publications, "Wells employed photographs as indisputable visual documents" that would counter any lingering doubts about the occurrence of lynchings and the horrible bloodletting that it entailed.[8] These publications repurposed lynching photographs not only to verify lynchings' numerous occurrences but, more important, to inspire horror at white aggression. In so doing, they called into question the designation of the black victims as "barbaric [and] inhumane" and instead cast enormous doubt upon the self-designation of the white mob and the nation overall as just and humane.

As this book maintains and Wells's strategies suggest, changing the way the image signifies means changing the character of the look that beholds it. Although that look called into question the humanity of the lynching actors, initially, at least, it did not entail engaging the black victim's humanity. That look, which I have called the look of humane insight, strives to see and recognize the body as human in order to condemn its violation. However, as historian Amy Wood explains, allegations of the lynching victim's criminal behavior—sometimes correct, sometimes not—threatened to solidify notions of black criminality.[9] Drawing any attention to the black lynching victim in antilynching tracts therefore proved to be a delicate affair. Even in the black press, which one might assume would be interested in drawing attention to the black victim of lynching, "captions regularly drew focus away from the corpse and onto the white perpetrators."[10] Indeed, much of the visual and verbal antilynching rhetoric of the early twentieth century avoided acknowledging the humanity of the victim, emphasizing instead lynching's destruction of American civility and morals. The spectacle of black suffering that so well served the abolitionist movement did not, at least initially, suit this new movement that had seen federal authorities look away from black bodies in the aftermath of emancipation. The failure of Reconstruction in which the civil rights of black citizens were sacrificed for the sake of white Southern power and prosperity materialized to African Americans the federal government's unwillingness to recognize them as human beings and citizens deserving of the state's protection.

The art gallery emerged as an important site in the battle against lynching practice and ideology. Addressing lynching's central dynamic—the spectacle of black suffering—the antilynching exhibition not only made the image of black suffering resignify as a sign of white (rather than black) inhumanity, but also drew upon the dynamics of looking in public—of being seen seeing—to authorize a specific way of looking at the black body in distress: looking with humane insight.

To begin this analysis of looking relations in the exhibition space, we must first acknowledge the peculiarities of the gallery environment in which the two antilynching shows were held. Nowhere is the photographed or painted body more privileged as an object-to-be-looked-at than in the art gallery. The modern "white cube," as it has come to be called, was thought to usefully minimize distracting elements and to offer a viewing environment unmarked by symbols of era, culture, and class. Yet as Fredric Jameson has noted, the ostensibly utopian gesture of deleting all signifying elements to create an ideally neutral space is itself mired in its own temporal, cultural, and classist preoccupations.[11] The traditional modern exhibition space—white-walled, windowless, minimally ornamented—does not really offer a neutral ground against which the "real" objects of aesthetic scrutiny can be seen. At least one scholar has posited that "by presenting objects as signifiers within an artificially created institutional frame, museums underline their irretrievable otherness, their separation from the world of lived experience."[12] In fact, the gallery space operates as an insidious guide, directing the viewers to the appropriate—but certainly not the only—objects of their gaze.

The viewing position that the exhibition space authorizes is an extremely restricted one that marshals its visitors to look deliberately at that which is positioned for display. The modern gallery does more than identify what objects are to be seen (the bust on the pedestal, but *not* the "Exit" sign in the corner); it also configures the discursive paradigms through which the objects are seen (the bust is art; the sign is an incidental architectural feature). The exhibition space participates knowingly but usually secretly in the work of designating how to look.

While the gallery space can and should be understood as ideological in its promotion of particular ways of seeing, the space cannot, in the end, absolutely determine the discourses that are invoked to understand and discuss a work, nor can it absolutely determine what the viewer sees. The two antilynching exhibitions are best understood when these authorized and unauthorized viewerships are acknowledged. Such a study makes for messy but important work in unpacking the *how* of the question "how does one look at images of violence?"

In foregrounding aesthetics as their purpose—that is, in insisting upon a proper way of beholding the object—the antilynching shows justify their presentation of lynching's counternarrative. This mission aligns the exhibition space with the writers and playwrights that Koritha Mitchell identifies as "groups [who] were invested in recording and preserving different kinds of evidence" about lynching and racial terrorism by mobilizing lynching to advocate for and testify to black perseverance and survival.[13]

Despite this admirable intention, the exhibitions grappled with the politics of graphically depicting the black body in pain and death. Like its print counterpart, the 1935 NAACP exhibition *An Art Commentary on Lynching* conveyed an uneasiness with, in particular, photographic documentation of lynching. The organization's 1935 antilynching pamphlet vividly illustrates this ambivalence by paradoxically reproducing a photograph of a lynching scene but also supplying the caption—explicitly an instruction to its viewers—"Do not look at the Negro. His earthly problems are ended."[14] The exhibition that was mounted that same year sidestepped the paradox entirely by electing to eliminate photographs from its showcase—a gesture that it could justify because of its claims that it provided an "art"—rather than documentary—commentary on lynching.

Timed to coincide with the appearance before Congress of the Costigan-Wagner antilynching bill, *An Art Commentary on Lynching* was a juried art exhibition designed to draw attention to the ongoing problem of unchecked lynching. The show's explicitly political aims speak to NAACP's understanding that the graphic arts—not only documentary artifacts and reports—could be effectively used to condemn lynching and defend the black body. *An Art Commentary on Lynching* was conceived by then executive secretary of the NAACP Walter White[15] who, in December 1934, addressed a letter to Gertrude Vanderbilt Whitney outlining his intentions for an art campaign against lynching and in favor of the antilynching bill. He explained that he was inspired by the success of "Mrs. [Pauline] Sabin [founder of the Women's Organization for National Prohibition Reform] and her co-workers [who] turned the tide of popular feeling against prohibition," and believed that "so can the sentiment be roused against lynching."[16] White went on to identify a number of works—Reginald Marsh's drawing *This Is Her First Lynching* (1934), John Steuart Curry's lithograph *The Fugitive* (1935), Julius Bloch's painting *The Lynching* (1932)—that "caused the idea [of the exhibition] to come into being." White also enclosed a "self-explanatory copy of an investigation of the recent Marianne, Florida, lynching." He added, somewhat self-consciously, that "[t]his, of course, seems and is morbid. But even a morbid subject can be made popular if a sufficiently distinguished list of patronesses will sponsor the exhibit and the right kind of publicity can be secured for it. . . . I am trying delicately to effect a union of art and propaganda."[17] To arts patron Suzanne La Follette, White put the matter more plainly.

> One of our biggest jobs is that of making opposition to lynching *more popular*. One of the ways of doing this is to take a leaf from the book written by Mrs. Sabin and her co-workers in getting *snooty society girls* and others to let it be known that they were opposed to prohibition.
>
> My idea is this: to hold an exhibit in one of the better galleries of paintings, lithographs, cartoons and sculpture dealing with the subject of lynching and to have a distinguished list of patronesses for the show.[18]

White emerges here as cognizant of the exhibit's role as propaganda and echoes his colleague W. E. B. DuBois's assertion that "all art is propaganda and ever must be, despite the wailing of the purists."[19] What is also apparent in White's prose and becomes evident in at least one of the show's reviews is an elitism and a sexism that troublingly renders the popularizing of the antilynching movement through art a dilettante's affair. White's appeal to finer, "feminine" aesthetic principles—his mention of female patrons (but inclusion of only one woman artist) and his attention to appearance; that is, the "better galleries" and focus on popularity—betrays an air of exuberance that fails to mirror the gravity of the subject matter. The organization's disengagement with the horror of lynching as a reality (as opposed to a theme) is further highlighted by its divergence from the antilynching exhibition hosted by Communist organizations that opened only two days after the NAACP exhibition closed.[20]

The NAACP exhibition's political aims and its dedication to art aesthetics raise questions about how we look at images of violence and how the aesthetics of violent imagery may be discussed. As we analyze the effectiveness of the exhibition, it is important that we consider the nature of its visual rhetoric. How is the horror that the works aim to effect shaped and determined by the type of media involved—drawings, paintings, and sculpture? To what extent do the representations—abstractions and interpretations—of actual lynchings convey the violation of black humanity?

Opening on February 15, 1935, at the Arthur U. Newton Galleries in New York City,[21] the exhibition featured during its two-week run works by prominent artists of many races, including Hale Woodruff, Peggy Bacon, and Isamu Noguchi, on the subject of lynching. Artists featured in the show strove to depict the act of lynching itself as politically intolerable and to portray the victim as a sympathetic human being by contrasting the inert body of the lynching victim with the portrayed frenzy of the lynch mob. Painter and draftsman Reginald Marsh's work *This Is Her First Lynching* (1934) elects to eliminate the lynched body altogether, focusing instead on the amassed crowd, its attention directed at something beyond the left-hand side of the frame. Just right of center of the image, held aloft by a woman with widened eyes and agape mouth, is the little white girl to whom the title of the image refers. The message conveyed by the drawing and its title is the loss of innocence being experienced by this girl and her induction into the community that finds pleasure in the spectacle of lynching.

According to art historian Dora Apel, by leaving out the black body at the heart of the lynching, Marsh's drawing, executed in black ink and crayon, "emphasizes lynching as a communal entertainment and makes visible the participation of [white] women, who were usually stereotyped as peace-loving and nurturing, and the initiation of children in acts of race terror."[22] Considering the exhibition overall, Apel remarks on the recurrence of artists' references to classical, mainstream aesthetic standards, which she regards as an attempt to associate the image of the victim of lynching with the image of an idealized, heroic masculinity.[23] As a consequence, the depictions of lynching were available to be scrutinized for their aesthetic value and visual technique rather than the evidentiary claims of lynching photography valued by the antilynching press. The nudity of the lynched figure in George Wesley Bellows's lithograph *The Law Is Too Slow* (1923), for instance, could be appreciated for its reference to neoclassical paintings and Greek sculptures of heroic males rather than the details it provides on the realities of lynching.[24]

Art-historical narrative and its determinations of art's priorities blunted the political urgency of the exhibit's ostensible mission. In fact, one might wonder why an exhibition with activist aims would be juried at all. In this case, competing interests conspired to deflect attention from the condition of tortured and murdered human beings on earth and toward a more existential and aesthetic consideration of the representational practices involved in depicting tortured and murdered human beings throughout the long history of art making.

Reviews of the exhibition reveal that the violation of black humanity was deemed too political to imbue the works with greater aesthetic value. In fact, reviewers encouraged looking away from the black body in order to appreciate the art for its artistic merit. Reluctantly declaring "moot" the "primary question of the right of such undiluted propaganda to be judged as an exhibition of art," the art journal *Parnassus* looked past the political and emotional implications of Allan Freelon's depiction of "a roasting negro" in the painting *Barbecue American Style* (1934) to conclude instead that "[t]he most interesting aesthetic point made by the show is the extent to which the use of identical subject matter has induced a similarity in quality and style regardless of the medium."[25] The *Parnassus* reviewer was comparatively generous in her willingness to discount politics in favor of aesthetic judgment. For another arts publication, *Art News*, the artistic engagement with a politically loaded topic was an offense that could not be overcome. That journal scathingly declared that in the NAACP exhibition, "[a]rt and propaganda have never to our memory been more unfortunately wedded" and "although the works of many talented artists are to be found, a strong atmosphere of sensationalism is the prevailing note."[26] Rather than imbue the artworks with valuable considerations of the human condition, the representation of the lynched black body confounded art reviewers at best and offended them at worst for its distraction from the universalist values of beauty and truth.

An extended and thoughtful review of the exhibit published by *New York Post* reporter Archer Winsten works through the aesthetic problem of the lynched black body. The article ultimately arrives at a qualified acceptance of the wounded black body's appearance in art by analogizing it to an accepted, traditional artistic subject—the martyrdom of Christian figures. Winsten, who was better known as a movie reviewer,[27] succinctly covers the range of responses reported by gallery visitors and other reviewers. Before even discussing the works themselves, Winsten reminds his reader that "it is one thing to deplore lynching, as who does not, and quite another to see it on the wall."[28] This proves to be a bad-faith distinction that confuses apolitical interpretation for an aesthetic history that is organically outside of politics. Nevertheless, he poses the reader a rhetorical question—"But it is another thing to look at the detail of a first-class lynching. Can't we be spared the revolting details?"—thereby inviting the reader to accept his skepticism and leave the issue of ideologically motivated murder out of their appreciation of the gallery tour.[29]

Winsten's question and his suggestion of the term *first-class* to describe lynching do more than echo White's elitist view of art. Rather, his prose bespeaks his fascination with hyperrealism, the vivid and evocative depiction of gore involved in the lynching ritual. The "revolting details" that he disdains are presumably those that appear dangerously and frighteningly real. The very notion that there could exist such a thing as a "first-class lynching" suggests that there are certain conventions to be fulfilled in the ritual of lynching; a notion that several researchers, who have identified castration as common in lynchings, have more or less corroborated.[30]

Winsten is clearly averse to these gruesome elements, whether real or depicted. The implied prudishness and propriety of his final question is mitigated, however, by his citation of a few choice words from Pearl Buck's speech at the exhibition opening, wherein she declared that "if one of these pictures for one moment brings any one a realization that behind every one of these pictures there is a reality—some one did so die at the hands of such a cruel horde—then we cannot spare these pictures."[31] Perhaps Winsten was himself swayed by Buck's estimation that "the pictures could not be too terrible if they portrayed lynching horrors as they really are."[32]

If neither he nor his readers finds Buck's claim compelling enough to foment the blending of "art and propaganda," they find at the end of the article yet another, perhaps more palatable, justification for viewing such work: the mantle of high art. In a conversation with the gallery owner Arthur U. Newton, Winsten is presented with what seems to be Newton's own aesthetic epiphany. Explaining how he himself stepped in to offer a space for the showing after another gallery backed out under the pressure of protest, Newton says,

> I thought the exhibition deserved to be shown. I feel it has real artistic merit, showing how many artists tackle the same problem. And then, too, it's still the crucifixion—the same problem so often treated by the old masters.
>
> Late this afternoon I had an inspiration about 3 o'clock. I remembered I had a Van Dyck lynching—"The Martyrdom of Saint Sebastian." It parallels these absolutely. I hung it in the other room. Perhaps you'd like to see it.[33]

With that remark, according to the author, Winsten followed Newton "[into] a rear room bathed in gentle light [where there] was the huge Van Dyck, valued at $25,000 and painted three hundred years ago. . . . The Saint looked inquiringly at you. There was no blood, no fire, no hemp at the neck. No agony."[34] Consistent with this notable absence of representations of gore and pain, neither Newton nor Winsten seems particularly concerned with the political causes of Sebastian's persecution and physical trauma (namely, his resistance to Roman law in pursuing Christian faith). Newton uses the term *lynching*—in a manner with which Winsten implicitly agrees—to draw attention to a stylistic parity with the nearby works representing the present-day persecution of blacks. In Winsten's transcription of the exchange there is no discussion of Sebastian's—unmentioned but understood—identity as a Christian nor of the injustice of his condemnation and execution by Roman edict. The unjust cause of Sebastian's "lynching" and the proof that it provides of a systemic and now deemed illegitimate prejudice against Christians do not figure in the interpretation of Van Dyck's painting as a representation of a lynching. Newton and, subsequently, Winsten recognize the painting as the representation of a lynching in solely visual and allegorical terms—at a remove from the emotionally invested and politically engaged terms delineated by humane insight—because it represents a man being made to suffer because of his religious identity and conviction. Newton and Winsten do not, however, make any mention of the illegitimacy of the persecution. In short, there is no indication in their exchange of humane insight—the recognition of humanity being violated.

This quaint conclusion to the article (mirroring the conclusion of Winsten's gallery visit) unsubtly explains to the reader (whose skepticism Winsten immediately assumes) why the artworks in *An Art Commentary on Lynching* are valuable as works of art. By comparing the subject of the seventeenth-century Anthony Van Dyck painting to the subject of the lynching show artworks, Winsten proclaims lynching to be an aesthetically viable subject of the plastic and graphic arts. The monetary and historical values associated with Van Dyck's painting of Saint Sebastian confer the aura of aesthetic value upon the works in *An Art Commentary on Lynching*. But if the Van Dyck can confer value upon these newer works, could these images of lynching also contribute an additional layer of meaning to the Van Dyck? Does the term *lynching*, as it is used by Newton, come to connote an aesthetic and compositional iconography separate from the physical violence of actual lynchings? Put another way, does the universalizing of lynching aesthetics undermine the political impetus behind Walter White's declared aims of the NAACP show—that is, to mobilize people against lynching?

Similar questions carry over into the more recent presentations of lynching images and objects. Addressing these questions requires a careful consideration of the exhibition space itself. The modern gallery setting in which the artworks of the NAACP show appeared influenced the kind of looking that Winsten and his fellow reviewers thought possible. The exhibition gallery configures visitors as welcome spectators who are invited to look and welcomed to pass judgment on images and objects. The gallery setting presents itself as a relatively safe place to look, one where intense scrutiny and even staring at the objects presented for display is accepted and encouraged. As such, the gallery presupposes a specific type of looking and designates particular objects as available to the look. Alongside the pressures of cultural codes and social sanctions, the exhibition space covertly contributes to designating how to look.

In recent years, images of lynching have been treated to gallery environments and cultural contexts that encourage—though they cannot guarantee—looking with humane insight upon the depicted victims of lynching violence. Exhibitions featuring images of lynching include *New York Divided: Slavery and the Civil War* (New York Historical Society, 2006–7); *The Struggle against Lynching* (The National Great Blacks in Wax Museum, permanent); *Silent Witness: Recent Work by Ken Gonzales-Day* (University of California at San Diego University Art Gallery, 2011); *Ahistoric Occasion* (Massachusetts Museum of Contemporary Art, 2007), which featured Kerry James Marshall's *Heirlooms and Accessories* (2002), a painting based on the well-known photograph of the Shipp-Smith lynching of 1930; and, most famously, *Without Sanctuary: Lynching Photography in America* (touring, ongoing).

The diverted looks of *An Art Commentary on Lynching* and the antilynching press differ significantly from the looks encouraged by these recent antilynching art shows that invite the viewer to look at and even identify with the lynching victim. Now that the threat of and approval for lynching is (seemingly) at an all-time low, humane insight emerges as the prevailing way of looking at lynching. The gallery space continues to be a space in which any number of looks is possible, including the look that takes pleasure in the spectacle of death. This pluralism recommends an examination of the multiple and sometimes competing looks that appear in the gallery settings and within the images themselves. An examination of authorized and unauthorized viewing positions provides us with a better understanding of how these modes of looking work and of the role of the suffering black body in influencing those looks.

Unlike the first half of the twentieth century, the present moment more readily encourages (not to say demands) that all people, regardless of racial identification, look with humane insight upon the black bodies represented in the image. With the terror of lynching at a historical remove, we are able to look with a sense of entitlement seemingly guaranteed by temporal distance and pity the deforming of both white and black humanity that the act of lynching encouraged. It would seem as though the dawn of the new century had permitted us the safety of a retrospective look at one of the most horrible episodes in American history.

But if the temporal abyss between the current-day gallerygoer and the moment documented in the lynching photograph is challenged, however, and the present-day viewer's connection to the past and to the bodies shown in the image comes into focus, the vicissitudes of humanity once again emerge, sometimes inspiring feelings of shame that threaten to overwhelm and challenge a righteous sense of one's own humanity. Further revealed is the naïveté of a belief that assumes that the passage of time has secured the safety of black humanity. Black people continue to be harassed by the anonymously placed noose that draws its power from its significance to lynching. In the act of looking, temporal boundaries are easily transgressed and historical remove is shown to offer no protection from the look that delights in spectacles of racialized violence.

For the most part, these recent exhibitions do not, in and of themselves, indulge in the bliss of historical amnesia nor do they indicate that we are securely ensconced in a world free of racist and white-supremacist looking practices. Rather, these exhibitions underscore our temporal, ideological, and emotional proximity to the images and the events of lynching. We continue to inhabit a world that invokes the visual discourse created by lynching. The current ideological environment insists (though it does not guarantee) that the photographs are viewed as documents of a time embodying convictions now thankfully lost to us. Nevertheless, it is imperative to remember that we read *through* history, not against it. The visual and political codes that informed the creation and the reception of lynching photographs are what make the images legible both then and now.

That said, in the present moment we are comparatively more equipped to accept the multiple ways that lynching photography circulates and is discussed. More than any other exhibit, *Without Sanctuary* elicited and engaged the competing looks to which lynching photography and exhibitions including lynching photography were submitted.

Without Sanctuary was first shown in New York with the title *Witness* and eventually traveled nationally and internationally.[35] In the show's various installations, the images were configured to operate as revelatory artifacts.[36] As a traveling exhibition, the organization of the photographs and other materials necessarily changed to conform to the particular demands of each location. Each location's curator was up against the potentially paralyzing notion that such images of violence were not amenable to an exhibition setting. Minimizing exploitation while maximizing reverence was an essential task of each venue's curatorial staff. A look at how individual venues addressed these problems exposes how spaces were designed to determine the onlookers' gazes.

At the Martin Luther King Jr. National Historic Site in Atlanta, where *Without Sanctuary* was on display from May 1 to December 31, 2002,[37] exhibition curator Joseph R. Jordan and designer Douglas Quin "attempt[ed] to create a reverential and respectful space that would make the exhibition both geographically and racially sensitive."[38] This move seems to have blunted critiques that feared the exhibition would reopen old wounds and harm relations between white and black Atlantans or that black visitors would be subject to revictimization. Ultimately, the King site presented the photographs alongside antilynching documents from the NAACP, Ida B. Wells, and the international press as well as the album cover of the 1992 Public Enemy EP *Hazy Shade of Criminal* that featured the image of a lynching.[39] Also included was a twelve-minute documentary film produced especially for the Atlanta venue further contextualizing the history of lynching in the United States, a wall mount of the Abel Meeropol poem "Strange Fruit," and a soundtrack that included Cassandra Wilson's and Billie Holiday's recordings of the song "Strange Fruit."

The expected emotional outpouring determined some of the curators' decisions regarding supplementary spaces and materials, such as constructing a "contemplation room" and, in a singularly empathic gesture, providing a box of tissues.[40] Although the careful construction of the exhibition indicates the curators' attempt to diminish the exploitative nature of the images by creating a respectful environment, that constructedness evidently did not diminish the affective power of the images. One journalist visiting the exhibit at the Martin Luther King Jr. National Historic Site in Atlanta reports seeing an elderly man, overcome with tears, rush hurriedly out of the exhibition.

The man, who turned out to be from Florida, later explained that when he was only one year old, his father had been lynched. The article explains that the man "had come to see if maybe there was a photograph of his father in the exhibit. But he just couldn't bear to stay."[41] Similarly, while the images were at the Jackson State University venue in Jackson, Mississippi, a man reportedly "ran from the building, his fist over his mouth, his eyes wet and his shoulders heaving."[42] The article provides no explanation for the man's hasty exit.

These visitors' emotional responses indicate quite clearly the impact that the act of looking can have on onlookers' emotions. Although this exhibition, unlike the 1935 antilynching show, does not position itself in an active antilynching campaign, it does figure itself as politically opposed to lynching. Whereas the purported project of the NAACP exhibition was to eliminate the occurrence of lynching, *Without Sanctuary,* though historically situated after the lynching epidemic, nonetheless assumes lynching as an issue, but as an abstract political issue rather than a politically pragmatic one. The historically displaced, twenty-first-century viewer has recourse to changing nothing but his or her own emotional and political disposition. What is at stake in the current antilynching exhibition is not the abolition of lynching but the interrogation of looking itself.

In *Without Sanctuary,* the exhibition environment influences the manner of looking and, by extension, the viewer's emotional response. As one reviewer writes, "One kind of viewing—very different from the kind that these photos originally elicited—is being sanctioned here . . . and it is worth thinking about the meaning of that difference."[43] The "kind of viewing" to which the reviewer refers is one in which the demand is on the spectator to adhere to the exhibit's implicit social code. Although, as Susan Sontag remarks, "there is no way to guarantee reverential conditions in which to look at these pictures and be fully responsive to them," the directives of the contextualizing objects and the gravitas of the subject itself subtly pressure the viewer to view the scene of lynching and especially the death of its main figure with a funereal respect.[44] As in the funeral setting wherein the deceased body is honored, *Without Sanctuary*'s visitor is compelled to look upon the body of the black victim with humane insight, calling to mind and honoring with the imagination the life that was so brutally extinguished. This recommended look is stated explicitly in the exhibit's objectives and reinforced by the fact that the viewing, occurring as it does in a public environment, is available for criticism itself. At the Charles H. Wright Museum of African

American History in Detroit, for example, one reporter noted that part of the "visually and emotionally" graphicness was due to the "hole in the wall between the exhibit where you can look through and see others, those like you and those different, who are sharing this experience with you."[45] This installation feature, which compels gallerygoers to act as both seeing subjects and seen subjects, is yet another environmental feature that illustrates the need to think about looking as an embodied practice. The look—like any utterance—is expressed from a specific body located in space and in time. That looking body is also, necessarily, a potentially looked-at-body.

The inverse truth—that bodies that are looked at are also bodies that look—is an important understanding that makes the spectatorial acts of seemingly passive African Americans legible as the radical interventionist acts that they are. Black looks, in particular black looks of humane insight, were among the first in the history of lynching to see in that hideous act not the spectacle of black criminality and racial shame but the unjust and untimely destruction of black human beings. Additionally, an attention to the black looks of lynching's victims, some of whom return a defiant gaze, works to disrupt the wholesale reading of lynching images as spectacles of black inhumanity. Such acts of black looking represented in lynching images complicate our appreciation of the viewing dynamics that are seemingly organic to the lynching spectacle. We need to consider the looks of the black people depicted within these images to make clear that it is not only the gallery space but also the image itself that challenges a narrow interpretation of itself as a scene of black unmaking.

Considering the black body as a seeing body rather than a body to be seen is itself a significant move. Looking is frequently aligned with autonomy and embodiment, two modes of subjectivity often denied to black subjects and especially to the black subjects of lynching.[46] Historically, the black body has been positioned as an object of visual pleasure, incapable of—or disabled from—resisting visual scrutiny. Both men and women of African descent have been stigmatized by a Western gaze that uses visible signs of difference to justify both hypersurveillance and visual disregard. The legacy of South African Saartjie Baartman, the so-called Hottentot Venus, and Congolese Ota Benga, both of whom were displayed in zoos and traveling exhibitions in the West, haunts the visual submission of black people today. In light of this history, to identify the black body as a "bearer of the look," especially in scenes of lynching, where all eyes are intended to be on the objectified black body, is a radical move.

The most striking appearances of black looks in lynching photographs are attributable to the victims of lynching themselves, those who are photographed while still alive. The few images from the *Without Sanctuary* collection that show living victims on the brink of death belong to two sets of photographs documenting their lynchings. Each photographic set concludes with the requisite image of the black man after he has died, indicating the desire of the original image owners and producers to commemorate their dominance over the black body.[47] Both of the photographic sets—one of Frank Embree, the other of Will James—seem to have been constructed to convey a narrative of the men's lynching and, in the case of the latter, the crime, pursuit, and capture that culminate in the final lynching.

The first photograph of the twelve-photograph Will James set appears to be a formal studio portrait. It is matched with photographs of

> the home of his alleged victim, Miss Anne Pelley; the home of the seven-year-old daughter of Mr. Boren, who found the murdered Miss Pelley in an alley she was crossing on the way to her grandmother's house; the "course the hounds took" [in pursuit of James]; the trains the mob took over to reach Belknap, Illinois, where James was apprehended, and to return him to Cairo for a public execution.[48]

Several of the images do not even include James, foreshadowing his body's ultimate obliteration by fire: one image (in two different versions) shows two rows of adolescent boys flanking what the caption explains are "the ashes of Will James." The living portrait stands apart from the others in the series because of its formalism. There, James is the only subject pictured, and neither the white background nor the plain oval frame that crops James at the chest and arms gives any indication of the circumstances under which the photograph was taken (although the date attributed to the photograph—1907—predates by two years the photographs of the lynching). Though the collector of this image, James Allen, claims that "Will James likely sat for this portrait at a local postcard photographer's studio," it is nevertheless impossible to discern whether the image represents a bourgeois desire to "metaphorically enshrine and quite literally perpetuate the example of [his] own identit[y]," as Henry Louis Gates Jr. has suggested of black portraiture, or if it is an example of "a scientific catalogue calling on the photograph as 'evidence' of African American inferiority," as Shawn Michelle Smith has argued with respect to bourgeois nineteenth-century African American photographic portraiture.[49]

Figure 1. Studio portrait of Will James circa 1907, Cairo, Illinois. Courtesy of the National Center for Civil and Human Rights, Atlanta, Georgia.

By contrast, other images in the series feature motion blurs and detailed landscapes. In one, the "half-burned head of James" on a spike is set against a peaceful background showing two-story middle-class houses situated among sparsely wooded, fenced yards. Such quotidian details—including, also, the motion blurs of restless children and dogs—indicate a dynamism and a situatedness that declares, unabashedly, that "this happened *here*."

Figure 2. Half-burned head of Will James on a pole in Candee Park on November 11, 1909, in Cairo, Illinois. Courtesy of the National Center for Civil and Human Rights, Atlanta, Georgia.

An arguably even more powerful (and disturbing) set of images features Frank Embree. Allen reportedly paid $30,000 for this three-card set of pictures displaying (1) a full-body shot of a naked Embree alive, facing forward, the cuts and blood from his recent whipping abundantly visible; (2) a full-body shot of Embree's back and wounds; and, lastly, (3) Embree, dead, hanging by his neck in front of a tree, with a cloth wrapped around his waist, and his open eyes trained skyward while the mob mills below. It is in the first photograph of Embree alive that the black gaze most strongly indicts the viewer as complicit in the spectacle of his lynching. *New York Times* art critic Roberta Smith sees in Embree's eyes the paradigm through which all other lynching photographs should be viewed. She writes,

> One exhibit at Roth Horowitz provides a glimmer of what these photographs might mean for the future. It is a photograph of Frank Embree standing on the back of a buggy, naked and chained, shortly before his death in Fayette, Mo., on July 22, 1899. He has been severely whipped and the camera records the deep lacerations up and down his body. But it also records his insuperable dignity and his eyes, which look down at the camera and directly into the lens, oblivious of the leering white men who crowd into the picture.[50]

Although Hilton Als's essay in the *Without Sanctuary* catalog contends that "Embree's eyes are dead," Smith counters that "it seems equally arguable that they know death is coming. Their narrow, exclusive focus gives them a flicker of life. Embree looks into the camera as if into the future, as if he knows that the camera will ultimately betray the men around him and let the world know his fate."[51] I agree with Smith's assessment that Embree's eyes do not seem "dead" as Als claims, yet I am not so sure about the prescience that Smith sees in Embree's eyes. This last vision seems to say more about Smith's desire than it does about the image itself. I do, however, notice several other things, including Embree's mouth (it is turned in what seems to be a sneer, conveying a note, even if unintended, of defiance), the composition of the photograph (Embree stands atop a wagon, his whole naked body on display, while the fully clothed white men stand behind the wagon and fill the picture's ground, their hats shading their eyes), and lastly that Embree is looking directly at the camera, his eyes at that moment focused on the photographer's camera (his head high, the opposite of the downward tilt that, psychoanalytic theorist Silvan Tomkins tells us, often indicates shame). This constellation of details tells me all too clearly that Embree was aware that his photograph was being taken and that he was aware it was being taken at his torturers' behest.

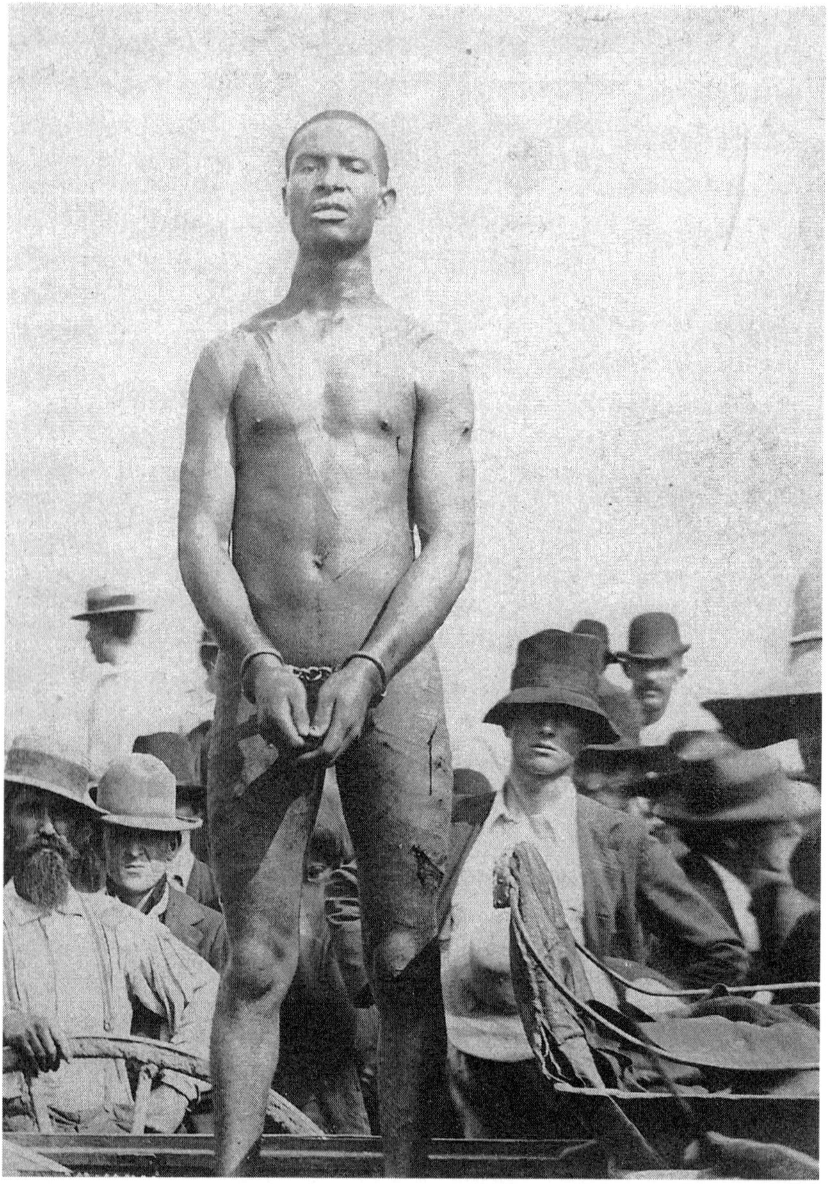

Figure 3. Frank Embree standing on a buggy, facing camera, on July 22, 1899, near Fayette, Missouri. Courtesy of the National Center for Civil and Human Rights, Atlanta, Georgia.

Of course, the purpose of taking this photograph was not to give Embree the opportunity offered to the present-day spectator to indict his photographer and soon-to-be killers with his eyes, even if that is the effect of his gaze today. Indeed, it was to preserve the image of Embree's lynching-in-progress so that the white community members who loathed Embree and his alleged crime, and supported his punishment, could memorialize their presence at the lynching or imagine it. In this respect, Embree is the main focus of this image, but only insofar as he solidifies the self-righteousness of the historical white onlooker. It is equally important that some of the white men who throng the photograph's foreground stare out from the image as well. Significantly, no one in this first photograph of Embree facing the camera is looking at Embree's body. They instead look, like Embree, directly into the camera lens. Their direct gazes balance Embree's; no viewer, either historical or current, can identify with or pity Embree without contending with the collective gaze of this self-righteous mob. In the white supremacist uses of this photograph, Embree's body is but the means of—and in some respects, the alibi for—the solidification of a community characterized by its belief in the righteousness of (this) lynching. Embree's body serves as the locus where the gazes of the mob and the looks of the displaced historical spectators meet. As both object and alibi, Embree's body provides the occasion for the present-day viewer's jarring and potentially uncomfortable encounter with the approving looks and beliefs of the mob.

In the second photograph in the series, Embree's back faces the camera. A few members of the crowd maintain their focus on the photographer's lens, but four men appear to be looking directly at Embree, now that he faces them. This photograph resonates profoundly with Maurice Wallace's assessment of the ideological underpinnings of photographing the black man from behind. The black man whose back faces the camera signals an "uncompromising rejection of the camera" wherein "the visual conditions of indeterminacy preserved by the anonymity of the man . . . suggest that black men suffer the double jeopardy of a *social and representational* sort simultaneously, . . . [and] powerfully demonstrate the photographic ways white people tend to look at black people in racialist societies."[52] In the photograph of Embree, by virtue of the white crowd situated *behind* the platform on which he stands, Embree is quite literally fixed within the sights of the masculinist white supremacist gaze. Given the conditions of the production of the photograph and the original audience of its circulation (in which a white audience is located literally behind and theoretically before him),

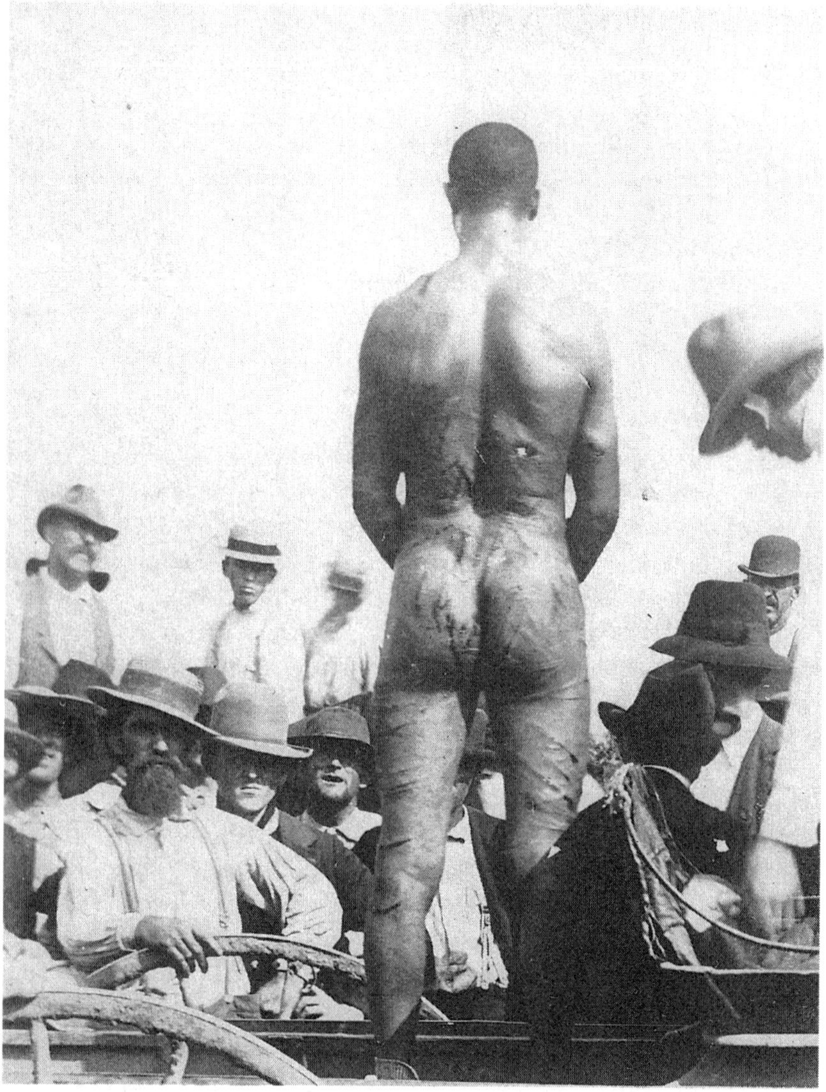

Figure 4. Frank Embree standing on a buggy, back to camera, on July 22, 1899, near Fayette, Missouri. Courtesy of the National Center for Civil and Human Rights, Atlanta, Georgia.

Embree is always both anonymous in his representation of a generalized (criminal) black manhood and individual in his identification as the specific subject of racist white scrutiny.

Embree's positioning between two gazes—that of the mob and that of the photograph's equally approving audience—is ultimately what underwrites the power of his gaze. By returning the gaze and not making of his body an object for unchallenged visual pleasure, his defiant look condemns those constituencies for taking interest in the spectacle of his body and its suffering. If the unifying white supremacist gaze of 1899 (the date of the photograph's production and of the lynching), distinguished by its self-righteousness, is enabled by the image of Embree's body as a mediating point, then by the same token, the antiracist twenty-first-century viewer's gaze is halted by Embree's gaze, unable (without, I argue, feeling ashamed) to complete the circuit that would acknowledge and affirm the proprietary gaze of the pictured mob. Embree does, in a manner, contradict the look of the mob with a look of his own—but not, I would argue, through his act of looking. Rather, his intent gaze into the camera lens extends to the photographer and to the photograph's imagined viewers who dare to delight in the image of his suffering.

Tragically, in the final picture in the series, Embree's gaze is, powerfully, undone. He is again at the center of the image, his body higher than that of the mob, only now he hangs by his neck from a tree, obviously dead. His eyes, however, remain open but unfocused in the grip of death. Perhaps this was an involuntary response. Or perhaps he kept his eyes open during his execution and died with a view of his surroundings and his fate. Either way, the final image does nothing to diminish the preceding depictions of black male embodiment, and embodiment that is indexed by the black subject's gaze.

Apart from Embree, James, and the numerous other black victims of lynching, there are other black subjects who populate, albeit sparsely, these photographs of racialized murder. They take up the role of spectators standing amid the overwhelmingly white crowds. The present-day viewer's discovery of a black body in the crowd of onlookers provides a moment of rupture in an otherwise easy equation of whites as bearers of the violent look and blacks as its powerless victims.

Images of African Americans attending lynchings do not afford unambiguous interpretation. In the Will James series is a photo of nine young boys who seem to be between the ages of eight and twelve flanking what

Figure 5. Frank Embree, dead and hanging in a tree on July 22, 1899, near Fayette, Missouri. Courtesy of the National Center for Civil and Human Rights, Atlanta, Georgia.

the text printed on the photograph states are the ashes of James. At least two of these boys are black. The black boys stand apart—one at the head of each flank—presenting their profiles to the camera. They seem at ease next to their white peers, suggesting a quaint, color-blind innocence of youth.

Another photograph, one that depicts the lynching of Jesse Slayton and William Miles on June 1, 1896, in Columbus, Georgia (an image that is not part of the *Without Sanctuary* collection), provokes similar consternation about the presence of three black subjects—this time adults—amid a large crowd of about twenty to thirty white onlookers. Again, the onlookers are positioned in two flanks, creating an alley in the photograph's center that ends at a tree from which two bodies—Slayton and Miles—hang. The crowd is composed predominantly of white adult males, though two young white boys look out from the edge of the right flank. The vast majority of the crowd members, including the three black adults, looks directly at

Figure 6. Slayton-Miles lynching, June 1, 1896, Columbus, Georgia. Photograph by Shipler Commercial Photography. Used by permission, Utah State Historical Society, all rights reserved.

the camera. On the left, partially obscured by the cropping of the image and the shoulder of the white man before her, a black woman (her gender signaled by her cloche-style hat) peers into the camera lens. Only a close examination uncovers that her eyes are opened wide and that her brow is slightly furrowed, indicating a note of discomfort. To her left, in the front row, stands a black man in loose work pants and a soft laborer's hat, his right hand resting on what seems to be a long-handled tool, perhaps a shovel. His right hand is in his pocket and, though he stands erect, his ill-fitting garments—and most significantly, the contrast between his clothes and the sharp suits, ties, and hats of the white men—make him appear comparatively powerless. His semirelaxed face, forming a stern mien similar to that of the white men to his right and left, does not convey the sense of self-righteousness evinced by the others, however. In another setting, this black man's posture and facial comportment could signify an intimidating glare.

A similar interpretation may be applied to the lone black man on the right who grimaces at the camera as though trying to deflect the sun's glare. He, too, betrays no sense of shame or discomfort that one might expect he would feel for being racially aligned with this spectacular policing of black criminality. In fact, his leaning into the picture (his head pops out at an acute angle from behind a white man's shoulder) suggests not just a fearlessness at being present but also a desire to participate in the moment and to have his presence documented. Clearly, this man does not see his presence in the audience of a lynching as a conflict of interest.

These three black adults—as well as the black children near James's ashes—convey their right to be present and to bear nonjudgmental witness to the lynching of black men. While a white man props up the head of one of the lynching victims in the background of the Slayton-Miles lynching photo, presumably to make the victim more visible to the camera, these living adults make themselves more visible. Although they probably understood (which is absolutely not to say they agreed with) their lowly station in relation to the white townsfolk, they do not appear to identify the racialized violence visited upon the two black men hanging from the tree as heralding a risk to their own bodies—at least not at this precise moment. In this last regard, as I shall explain, lawfulness has apparently trumped race in the consolidation of a notion of shared humanity.

The black adults looking away from the bodies of the dead black men suggests a failure if not a refusal by these adults to identify with the lynched black bodies. Instead, the three appear to indulge in the pleasure of their own embodiment, identifying simply as audience members at a significant local event. *Disidentification* may be called upon here to explain the protective work that looking away conducts for the minority subject. José Muñoz defines and deploys the term to describe "the survival strategies the minority subject practices in order to negotiate . . . a public sphere that continuously elides or punishes the existence of [minority] subjects."[53] In this instance, shared racial identity is not enough to forge what is recognizable (to us) as a racially determined collective that understands the experience of being black as the experience of being a subject of trauma. These adults' gestures of looking away from a seemingly obvious point of identification—the race of the lynched men—imply a refusal to identify with this particular instantiation of black victimization and, perhaps more to the point, of black criminality in favor of a commitment to their own protective sense of embodiment. In fact, the linking of blackness and trauma (a connection that I find elsewhere to be very helpful and apt) may be just what explains the evident aversion of these photographed black adults to identifying with the lynched black men. In short, these adults may be very understandably ignoring the prospect of racial identification in order to avoid absorbing the trauma of black vulnerability that lynching invokes. Their presence among and their identification with the other lynching onlookers might be justified as an attempt at a deracialized self-affirming identification that seeks, as its primary goal, psychic health and, in psychoanalytic terms, wholeness.

What may well override the black spectators' identification with the black victims here and in other instances of lynching is the intervening detail of the victims' (accurate or contrived) configuration as criminals. This last point recommends yet another reading of the photograph as one not ostensibly distinguished by race, but by a hard-and-fast distinction between the law-upholding (the black and white mob) and the lawless (the lynched black men). In this case, it is shame and its associate affect—disgust—and the gestures of overcompensating for these affective attachments that define the relationship between the black spectator and the black victims. Lest one be inclined to remove any racial reading of this image, however, I add that these other terms—*lawlessness* and *lawfulness*—are themselves racially coded, a legacy of the de jure criminalizing of blackness that originated in the wake of emancipation, when African Americans who "often had nowhere to go . . . found themselves designated *trespassers, disturbers of the peace, vagrants, or loiterers.*"[54]

Just as the body may signify spatial transgression, so too may the look signify a critical one. The look can function like the body of the loiterer, lingering too long in a particular place and refusing to announce its intent. The loiterer is someone whose persistence and secretiveness are amenable to an unhurried and potentially disruptive encounter with images and objects. As Susan Sontag explains, the materials on the walls and in the cases at the gallery "are stations along a—usually accompanied—stroll."[55] But unlike the bourgeois flaneur who indulges his leisure with careless strolls and disinterested glances, the loiterer looks with serious but undeclared interest at discrete objects until his dangerous presence is challenged. Moreover, according to its legal definition, the loiterer is also an illicit subject who, like trespassers and disturbers of the peace, has no right to be there. Yet unlike those two illegal subjects, the loiterer is not figured as an active transgressor of social norms. On the contrary, his (scopic) violations are incidental (perhaps even accidental), resolutely passive, and, despite this inaction, nevertheless recognized as criminal.

It is in this configuration of the illicit viewer that the disruptive look of humane insight begins to take shape. In the present-day viewing of photographs of lynchings, the viewer is well aware that he or she is not the lynching photographers' and lynching participants' ideal viewer. The gallery, too, with its encouragement of an antilynching stance does not constitute what the image makers envisioned as an ideal viewing environment. But even more incisive and fundamentally disruptive than the disapproving look is the look that perceives not only the humanity of the black victim but also wrestles with the humanity of the white lynchers.

Looking back on these photographs of unfathomable violence and reprehensible pride, we observe that when humane insight brings the humanity of the lynching victim into view, the humanity of the lynchers tends to get lost. The protective gesture that divides the world cleanly but inauthentically into good and evil leads us to characterize the lynching perpetrators and their equally self-righteous peers as monsters whose humanity lies beyond our comprehension. This is a dangerous elision as it threatens to install a newly configured antihumanist paradigm, this one in the name of antiracism, that would supplant the practices but repeat the strategies of racism. It is here, in the space where any inkling of human-as-human recognition might slip away, that the danger to the social body lies.

Viewing the lynchers with humane insight is a difficult and even distasteful task. It is nevertheless an important one as it distinguishes the viewers' capacity for humanity from the incapacity of the lynch mob. It is not so unseemly to identify with the suffering endured by the lynched black body. Heralding the danger that an exclusive identification with the lynched body entails, Carrie Rentschler remarks that such a move "allows people to claim their own sense of injury—from wherever that sense may come—in a way that forecloses their own accountability for violence they help perpetuate, often unknowingly but not always."[56] And yet, it is the intractability of the photographed lyncher and lynching spectators that is referenced in relation to the ironic and dangerous banality of lynching. As Leon Litwack writes in his essay for the *Without Sanctuary* catalog, "It is far easier to view what is depicted on these pages as so depraved and barbaric as to be beyond the realm of reason. That enables us to dismiss what we see as an aberration, as the work of crazed fiends and psychopaths. But such a dismissal would rest on dubious and dangerous assumptions."[57] The "dubious and dangerous assumptions" to which Litwack refers are not so difficult to imagine. The danger is based on the mistake of thinking that we are no longer intrigued or even pleased by the spectacle of another's pain. It is dubious because there exists much evidence that we regularly indulge in such spectacles, from the anecdotal seductive visual appeal of the car wreck to abiding endeavors of the applied arts, from film to classical painting, that represent death and suffering in graphic detail.

Although the consumption of images of suffering, violence, and death for personal pleasure is an abiding and troubling phenomenon, I do not believe that we can only understand this mode of looking in terms of pleasure. I also do not believe that a discrete, objective viewing position is at all possible because critical looking and scholarship are themselves situated and implicated in social relations and political perception. What we need instead is to consider the other responses that these images call for, such as a viewing position that polices itself. Shame can usefully intervene in the practice of looking, providing us with the tools both to acknowledge our intimate relationship with a past we would rather forget and to move productively into a future in which there are fewer atrocious public episodes like slavery and lynching.

To accomplish this task, it helps to think of the social body as a self, one that continually questions and corrects itself. Sociologist Thomas Scheff, in his work on shame, nationalism, and war, foregrounds the utility of shame as a social project: "Just as fear automatically signals a threat to the safety of our *physical self* (our bodies), so shame automatically signals a threat to the safety of our *social self*, the person that we think we are and expect others to think we are. We need to feel connected because the self is a social product, just as the body is a biological one."[58] Scheff's analyses of shame and of the "social self" are shaped by an investment in well-being—here, the well-being of the social self.

Sociology is not the only discourse interested in shame and society. Psychoanalyst Silvan Tomkins discusses shame in terms of behaviorism. He concludes that essential to the experience of shame is the initial experience of "interest." In their more recent resuscitation of Tomkins's work, Eve Sedgwick and Adam Frank explain that "[w]ithout positive affect there can be no shame; only a scene that offers you enjoyment or engages your interest can make you blush. Similarly, only something you thought might delight or satisfy can disgust."[59] The delight is signaled by the lynching crowd that unabashedly presents itself to an imaginary approving eye. The comportment of the lynching crowds that are seen in these photographs show a group composed predominantly of white men who pose, smile, and assume dignified countenances. The gazes into the camera lens and out of the photograph's surface assume our approval of their attitudes. The evident absence of their shame can be keenly felt by present-day viewers who, amazingly, can take on themselves the responsibility of shame for these distant actions. Remarkably, a viewer fifty or more years removed from the event can take up the second stage of the shaming sequence that Tomkins identifies, feeling in his or her own body an essential wrongness, what Elspeth Probyn calls a fundamental "out-of-placeness" that "make you want to disappear, to hide away and to cover yourself, [and] is felt in the rupture when bodies can't or won't fit the place—when, seemingly, there is no place to hide."[60] As Probyn goes on to explain, "Shame, as the body's reflection on itself, may reorder the composition of the habitus, which in turn might allow for quite different choices."[61] Looking at lynching photographs, then, might cause the out-of-placeness—that is, the political unacceptability—of the lynching act to manifest a discomfort in the politically engaged viewer. Shame destabilizes one's comfort with one's self and can prompt a reassessment that leads to a critique of social habits such as the endorsement of lynching. This critique need not be a despairing gesture, however, and we need not fear that looking at an image of atrocity and seeing in the perpetrators evidence of humanity will paralyze us with shame. In fact, looking with a universal application of humane insight can better distance both our viewing and our ideological positionings from the bigoted selective humanism practiced in lynchings.

The dissonance created by images of pain housed in a space dedicated to their viewing threatens to lead to exploitation. And yet, with respect to the lynching photographs, it is the way that the gallery makes the photographs signify as images for public perusal that contradicts and undermines their previous exploitative function as images for the private consumption of white supremacists. In this respect, the presentation of lynching photographs in the "inappropriate" space of the gallery has greater potential to produce "the equivalent of a sacred or meditative space in which to look at" such images.[62]

A significant choice is made when the viewer declines the invitation to share in the pleasure the lynch mob feels at the spectacle of black suffering and death. The faces of the lynch mob in the photographs greet viewers in this way, assuming a unified pleasure in the gaze of white power, just as they once greeted the photographer who photographed them. The photographs themselves would never have existed had he—the photographer—not taken up their ideological perspective—a perspective that produced and forever frames the photographs taken—along with his camera.[63] The mob, by way of the photographer, invites the viewer to look at the spectacle they created through the act of lynching and their desire to preserve an image of that act through photography—an invitation that most of us refuse. As has been argued previously via the application of a theory of shame as an adaptive affect, we might be moved to feel disappointed that people we would otherwise recognize as human beings—the mob—people presumably holding similar rational and ethical standards, could produce and, through the photographic process, *re*produce such an outrageous event. The irony, then, is that an act created to disfigure the black body could make the other bodies—the white bodies that predominantly comprise the lynch mob and the black lynching witnesses—unrecognizable, too.

Many looks inhere in lynching spectacles and representations. Depending on the context, a particular kind of looking is privileged and compels the recognition of certain bodies as human. The application of human identity to subjects is not an anterior truth but a discursive power, one that lynching, as an event, used to make obvious the presence and potency of white humanity as it obliterated the possibility of black humanity. Although the antilynching rhetoric as expressed in publications and exhibitions managed to unmoor the image of lynching from its signification of white supremacy and black submission, the more inclusive and indeed more difficult look of humane insight is better equipped to challenge the exclusive application of humanity that underwrites the bigotry of racialized violence. In achieving humane insight, we must hold in abeyance the spectacle of white terrorism alongside the image of the black body in pain.

3

Emmett Till, Justice, and the Task of Recognition

The act of looking is not only central to the political constitution and manipulation of humanity as the contexts of slavery and lynching reveal. It is also essential to the constitution and manipulation of identity. Involving self-constitution and self-presentation, identity is managed internally, through psychological processes, and externally, through the use of language and symbols. The project of black liberation that this book has traced thus far entails the humane insight of the state and of individuals in positions of relative power. Such insight effects the bonding of the onlooker to the beholden in a relationship of shared humanity. But how does one form such an important bond with another—especially another that the rhetoric of race has stigmatized as the Other—so absolutely and fundamentally distinct from the self?

Recognition is the tool that brings another being before our consciousness and permits us to bestow him with rights and care. In both its political and emotional uses, the act of recognition fundamentally shaped the way that one black boy's death influenced African American identity and civil rights activism in mid-twentieth-century United States. The revelation of Emmett Till's brutal murder and his horribly disfigured corpse drew a striking ideological line between those who refused to recognize black life and victimization and those who recognized the violated humanity and unwarranted suffering that begat Till's death and their own haunted black lives.

Recognition is an essential component to understanding the Emmett Till case. The task of recognition is not only restricted to identifying the dead black body as human, to humane insight; it is also primarily engaged with identifying whose body is represented—a project that implies the questioning of racial and evidentiary visual identification. Echoing the "danger" implied in the previous chapter regarding the paucity of documentary associations with graphic and plastic images, the danger that underwrites this entire project of recognition—that the image of the black body will not be recognized as human—is exacerbated in the Till situation as a result of the decomposition of Till's corpse. The recognition of Till's particular body is not only a recognition of his (black) body's humanity, but also a recognition and an acknowledgment of Till's identity as a son and as a black child—two terms that figure his body in specific ways in the various venues—the morgue, the funeral, the courtroom, and the mass media—that it appeared.

The public spectacles—of the funeral, the courtroom procedure, and the final tabloid confession—that distinguished Emmett Till's murder at the hands of at least two white men in 1954 provide the opportunity to mine the look's underlying structures for basic information about how we constitute ourselves and others. Exploring those structures leads us to appreciate the important work of recognition and the role of identity in bringing to light a defensible black humanity. By tracing the character of the many looks of the prosecution, of the defense, of Till's mother and uncle, and of a sympathetic mass media audience, one can better understand how a single image of a dead and tortured black body may serve opposing viewpoints.

The Murder

The reopening of Till's case by the Federal Bureau of Investigation in 2006 still contains several contested elements, including how many people were involved in the actual abduction and murder. The crux of the story, however, maintains that in August 1955, fourteen-year-old Emmett Louis Till of Chicago, Illinois, was visiting his great-uncle Moses "Mose" Wright, a sharecropper, and other relatives in Mississippi on a summer vacation. Although the details of the encounter are still debated, what is known is that Till had some interaction with a white female shopkeeper, then twenty-one-year-old Carolyn Bryant, at her family store in the small town of Money in Leflore County, Mississippi. Three days later, at 2:30 A.M. on Saturday, August 28, 1955, Bryant's husband, Roy Bryant, twenty-four; brother-in-law, J. W. Milam, thirty-six; and, according to many accounts, one or two others (including, perhaps, Carolyn Bryant herself) drove to the home of Moses Wright to abduct Till. Till was taken to Milam's toolshed, where he was beaten. The beating was overheard by an eighteen-year-old black man named Willie Reed who eventually testified at the trial. At some point, Bryant and Milam apparently decided to kill Till. They found a cotton-ginning fan and drove to the edge of the Tallahatchie River, where they say they shot Till in the head, then secured the seventy-pound fan to his neck with barbed wire and threw his body into the river.[1]

Following its discovery on August 31, 1955, Till's body was loaded with racial and legal significance by politicians, local police, and a predominantly black press that recognized the multiple resonances of this singular death. The body was found by a seventeen-year-old white boy, Robert Hodges, who spotted feet sticking out of the water at Pecan Point in the Tallahatchie River. By that time, local Mississippi law enforcement had been made well aware of Till's abduction and disappearance: Moses Wright and his brother-in-law, Crosby Smith, had notified their local sheriff, George Smith, the morning after the abduction, and Chicago police, contacted by Till's mother, Mamie Till, thirty-three, alerted Tallahatchie County Sheriff Harold Clarence Strider. (There are also accounts claiming that Till's cousin, Curtis Jones, also from Chicago, called Sheriff Strider directly to report the kidnapping.) When the body was retrieved from the river and taken to the undertaker, it was so badly decomposed that it could only be identified by a signet ring that bore the initials "L. T."—the initials of Louis Till, Emmett's estranged father. Ostensibly due to the condition of the body, Strider ordered that Till's body be buried immediately, but Jones intervened by phoning Mamie Till in Chicago and notifying her of Strider's order. Mamie Till's own assessment of the situation was that "the main thing [the police in Tallahatchie wanted] to do was to get that body in the ground so nobody could see it."[2] She insisted that her son's body be returned to Chicago. It was, but only on the condition set by the sheriff's office that the casket never be opened. The box containing Emmett Till's body arrived at the Illinois Central rail terminal in Chicago on Friday, September 2, 1955.

The Mother

The arrival of Emmett Till's coffin and the subsequent opening of the coffin—in defiance of a contract agreed to by the Chicago funeral director A. A. Raynor and Mississippi officials—marked the beginning of a struggle for recognition of the body that would carry over, in different ways, into several disparate domains, including the funeral viewing and the courtroom case.[3] Great efforts had been taken to ensure that the body would never be seen. When the murderers' attempt to conceal the body in the river failed, local officials stepped in to fulfill the task. When it became apparent that the body of Emmett Till would have to be returned to his mother, the state coroner packed the body in lime to accelerate its decomposition and took the extra step of legally locking the box shut with the seal of the State of Mississippi.[4]

But when the coffin arrived, Mamie Till flouted the edicts and demanded that Raynor open the coffin so that she could see and check the remains. As she explains in her autobiography,

> I was not bending. That box had to come open. I mean, I didn't even know what we would find inside. There could have been bricks, mud, someone else's body. I would spend the rest of my life not knowing. Besides, I had heard so many things over the past couple of days, I had to see for myself what they had done to my son.[5]

In her own words, her need to see and to recognize her son was necessary, not optional. We can intuitively understand this response as the desire of a mother to bestow upon her deceased son the caring look of humane insight. Yet another explanation connected with the work of mourning permits us to extrapolate from this specific occasion of death an understanding of the visual encounter with the dead body as a project of compassionate responsibility.

In demanding that the box be opened, Mamie Till articulates a logic explained by Jacques Derrida as the responsibility of the living to the dead. Contemplating the legendary onus encapsulated by Hamlet and Antigone, two literary characters whose motivations are entirely propelled by their imagined responsibilities to their kin, Derrida offers that "[n]othing could be worse for the work of mourning, than confusion or doubt: one *has to know* who is buried where."[6]

However, as Till's mother soon discovers, the task of recognizing her son's body is not easy. In the Chicago funeral home, Mamie Till's visual project of bestowing a particular humanity—her son's—on this body is influenced by her identity as a mother, an identity that in turn gives the task of recognition the great urgency underscored by Derrida. But her task is frustrated by the body's visual appearance. At a speech given shortly after Till's murderers' acquittal, Mamie Till admitted that "[w]hat I saw in that box was not like anything I've ever seen before in my life."[7] The detailed description of that initial visual encounter that she offers in her memoirs is wrenching.

> When I got to his chin, I saw his tongue resting there. It was huge, I never imagined that a human tongue could be that big. . . .
>
> From the chin I moved up to his right cheek. There was an eyeball hanging down, resting on that cheek. . . . Right away, I looked to the other eye. But it wasn't there. . . . Dear God, there were only two [teeth] now, but they were definitely his. I looked at the bridge of his nose. . . . It had been chopped. . . .
>
> From there, I went to one of his ears. . . . And that's when I found out that the right ear had been cut almost in half. . . . And I don't know what happened to that part of his ear, but it wasn't on the back part of his skull. I did check. And when I did, I saw that someone . . . had taken a hatchet and had cut through the top of his head, from ear to ear. The back of his head was loose from the front part of his face. . . . I saw a bullet hole slightly back from the temple area. . . . [I]t was that one bullet hole that finally caused me to speak.
>
> "Did they have to shoot him?" I mean, he had to be dead by then.[8]

Her thorough inventory of body parts represents an attempt to metaphorically reassemble the vision before into the body of a unified and recognized human being.

Equally compelling as the encounter that Mamie Till narrates is the language that she uses to describe the encounter. One of her explications of the looking process merits especially close examination for the ways it engages and extends our understanding of how the visual image is connected to identity. In her autobiography, Mamie Till writes, "At a glance, the body didn't even appear human. I remember thinking it looked like something from outer space, something you might see at one of those Saturday matinees. Or maybe that's only what I wanted to think so that I wouldn't have to admit that this was my son."[9] Mamie Till's language here is fascinating in its seamless discussion of looks that constitute knowledge. Her invocation of cinematic metaphor—her reference to "Saturday matinees"—recalls psychoanalyst Jacques Lacan's use of the concepts *screen* and *gaze,* concepts that, along with *identification,* continue to prove integral to cinema studies and to psychoanalysis.

To briefly review the relevant points of Lacan's theory of identity: Individuals come to know themselves through the establishment of identities that are relatable and understandable to other people. This process of identification—that is, the process of attaching a coherent image of a Self to one's own Self—is defined by Lacan as "the transformation that takes place in the subject when he assumes an image."[10] This transformation or process is not only essential to the Self's ability to utilize language as a means of self-protection and self-fulfillment, but is also always an imperfect project as it necessarily smoothes over inconsistencies and imperfection in order to create a coherent identity.

Mamie Till's project of recognition as she stands before her son's damaged body is first and foremost to reconstruct from the disfigured body something recognizable as that of her son so that his identity can be restored anew. But the challenges she faces in the task are huge, and the reassembling of her son's identity requires not simply a rote gesture of visual recognition, but also an imaginative recognition, one spawned by looking but spurred on by love. She must look with not only humane insight, but also with a mother's insight to recognize and eventually mobilize the identity of this ruined body as that of her son, Emmett Till.

The looking that Mamie Till conducts is not only underwritten by a desire to recognize a human being, a desire that characterizes humane insight, but also by a desire to recognize someone she loves. Her act of humane insight is amplified by the love bond that grants the task of recognition its extreme urgency. Psychoanalyst Jessica Benjamin explains that the uniquely affective love bond, especially the version that forms between the mother and the infant, can have the effect of constituting both subjects through what Benjamin calls "mutual recognition."[11] In Benjamin's model, a subject comes to understand herself as an autonomous (if incomplete) being in the world "by being with another person who recognizes her acts, her feelings, her intentions, her existence, her independence."[12] But the role of recognition in constituting the Self does not end here, for, as Benjamin tells us, recognition is "reflexive; it includes not only the other's confirming response, but also how we find ourselves in that response," adding, "We recognize ourselves in the other."[13]

By privileging love over antipathy, Benjamin rewrites the dialogic of recognition instigated by German philosopher Georg Hegel that has informed and hobbled our understanding of human interaction and power. As Hegel asserts in his contemplation of human consciousness and intersubjective relations, the immediate response to perceiving another being possessing a conscious mind is to vanquish and eliminate that other. Whence this belligerence emerges Hegel fails to say, only offering that it is the power of each to kill the other that stays both hands and results in stalemate. The insertion of unequal power relations into this scheme complicates the work of recognition but does not remove its bitterness and venality. In the "Lord and

Bondsman" dialectic, both parties rely on the other for assurances of identity. The bondsman is, quite famously, an identity in "negativity," a consciousness that exists not for itself but for the other. Only when the bondsman is able to perceive that the absolute nature of his existence, an existence characterized by service and fear, is not only beholden to the lord but instead to the Lord—a conceptual move that indicates an appreciation of what Hegel calls "the absolute"—is the bondsman truly free. The solution that Hegel saw in the divine is the solution offered by Mamie Till—a bestowing of recognition not by the Father and the Son, but by the mother.

If recognition is based on love rather than animosity, then the kind of recognition that Mamie Till articulates is a model for the compassionate recognition that illustrates the productive and even activist work that looking can involve. It is not misrecognition, then, but the humane insight that animates her son's identity and allows for mutual recognition that engenders Mamie Till's compassion for the physical circumstances of her son's corpse and demise. The animating recognition enacted by Mamie Till registers in Lacanian terms as a fundamental but inevitable mistake. In the Lacanian system, when Mamie Till identifies with her son and registers the marks of pain and suffering evident on his body as tangible to her own, she is making a fundamental, albeit productive, mistake. But it is this "mistake" that constitutes the mechanics of humane insight. Enacting the reflexive component of mutual recognition outlined by Benjamin, Mamie Till "recognizes" herself in the body of her son.

Mamie Till's humane insight is significantly informed by her ability to perceive via the spectacle of her son's injured body her own body's potential response to torture. Mamie Till is compelled to think of her own body and her own body's limits when she takes visual account of her son's evident torture and murder: "I paused at the knees. They weren't knobby knees, they were nice, fat, round knees and rather flat. And they were *my* knees."[14] Unlike the torturer, who Elaine Scarry tells us in her landmark research on the logic of pain is "so without any human recognition of or identification with the pain that he is not only able to bear its presence but able to bring it continually into the present, inflict it, sustain it," Mamie Till can see herself in the body of the tortured and imagine herself in her son's place.[15] Her alignment of her body with his reaches its peak when she is able to identify with his sense of fear as she discovers, suddenly, that she might be able to see with his eyes. Riding in a taxi on the night of the trial's conclusion, passing through Mississippi back roads, Mamie Till recounts that she "was terrified and could only imagine the horrors that lay around every turn. And then an even more terrifying thought rushed over me: Was this what Emmett saw, was this what he thought on his last ride in Mississippi in the pitch black of night?"[16] It is by seeing what Emmett most likely saw that she is able to comprehend the depths of his fear.

The Community

The recognition and identification of Emmett Till's corpse was freighted at every step with implications and even dangers that could affect, one way or the other, every black person with whom he came into contact. Even the decision of when and where to admit to recognizing the disfigured body of Emmett Till as a human body, and as that of Till specifically, bore serious implications in the segregationist South. In a sad repetition of the injunction placed upon slaves not to betray their misery to inquisitive white eyes, the body's discovery precipitated moments when the psychic pain of recognizing the body could not be signaled to those in power.[17] This act of self-preservation—to conceal the experience of pain and vulnerability—temporarily thwarted the political project of making human vulnerability recognizable, but was a trade-off that was absolutely understood by Emmett Till's uncle Moses Wright, who was summoned to identify the body upon its discovery. Rather than let multiply the white dominance made visible during the lynching and repeat the act of submission-under-duress in another location (the morgue), when called to identify Emmett's body, Wright revealed no emotion and behaved in accordance with what Mamie Till calls "the code."

> He and every other black person in the Delta knew it and lived by it. Never show emotions. You couldn't show joy. That would be suppressed. You couldn't show anger. That would mean defiance. You couldn't show sorrow. That would mean weakness. I guess as far as Southern whites were concerned, blacks had no feelings.
>
> So Mose . . . dammed up his feelings, as he was so used to doing, holding back until later, until he couldn't hold back any longer.[18]

The emotions that Wright refused to express during the identification were to become, however, foundational to the political movement that Emmett Till's death and public funeral portended. It is the radical difference between black emotion in the morgue and black emotion during the funeral service that makes this case so remarkable in terms of the politics of affect and what Derrida calls "the work of mourning." Both sites stage, each in its own way, the importance of recognizing the right body at the right time and in the right way.

The Mourner

Mamie Till orchestrated a political event by inviting a viewing public to an open-casket funeral where they would behold the devastated body of her son. In staging the event, she sought to make universally recognizable and undeniable both her and her son's pain. In a speech delivered shortly after the acquittal of her son's murderers, Mamie Till explained what motivated her decision—her own first view of his corpse. Only moments after seeing Emmett's corpse for the first time,

> I said, "Roy [Mooty, Mamie Till's cousin], anybody that wants to look at this, can see it. I'm tired of stuff being covered up." If some of these lids had been pulled off of Mississippi a long time ago, then something like this wouldn't be happening today. So far as my personal feelings are concerned, they don't count. . . . And if my son had sacrificed his life like that, I didn't see why I should have to bear the burden of it alone. There was a lesson there for everybody.[19]

Emmett's body lay in state for four days at the Roberts Temple Church of God. The church was thronged by visitors, primarily by black Chicagoans, who had followed the story of the kidnapping and murder through the black press and the mainstream media outlets. Implicitly, it seems, Mamie Till understood the political possibilities of making her son's body visually available to a public already aware of the ongoing threats against black life in the South. Her belief was that, in confronting the disfigured body of Emmett Till, "people also had to face themselves. They would have to see their own responsibility in pushing for an end to this evil."[20] Seeing the brutality enacted upon the body of a young black boy would perhaps make the country acknowledge just how dire the situation was for African Americans in the American South.

Mamie Till understood the power of looking to do what words could not. Her decision to have a public, open-casket funeral and to guarantee that both the funeral and the body were photographed stem from an understanding that people "had to see what I had seen. The whole nation had to bear witness to this. . . . I knew that if they walked by that casket, if people opened the pages of *Jet* magazine and the *Chicago Defender*, if other people could see it with their *own* eyes, then together we might find a way to express what we had seen."[21] It seems that even the transformation of the task of looking into a task of recognition—a task whose terms are not only expressed in the language of emotion but also in the language of justice—demonstrates the importance of the image in contesting the validity of unrestrained brutality.

Knowing that the viewing public—the mourners—had little if anything to compare to Emmett after his torture and death, Mamie Till provided photographs of Emmett while alive for comparison. The viewing of the body was thus an orchestrated affair, relying in part on the juxtaposition of visual objects to make its political and affective points. At the viewing, the painful reality that a young black boy's body could endure such violence that it became difficult to recognize that body as human let alone as Emmett Till was underscored by the photographs taken during Emmett's last Christmas with his family that were taped to the coffin lid.

The juxtaposition of the photographs that represented Emmett Till alive and the dead body made an emotional appeal to a sentimental aesthetic more commonly associated with memorial photography of nineteenth-century America. At that time, the photograph was a central feature in the mourning process, and in fact these memorial photographs constitute the largest group of nineteenth-century American genre photographs. As collector Stanley Burns explains, "Surviving families were proud of these images and hung them in their homes, sent copies to friends and relatives, wore them as lockets or carried them as pocket mirrors."[22] The most disturbing images of this genre are also the rarest; they are the premortem photographs. In the earliest days of photography, when most people did not have their portraits taken, photographers appealed to customers with the slogan "Secure the Shadow Ere the Substance Fade," which united the unpredictability of death with photography's technical ability to freeze time, as it were, in the image. After a person had fallen ill, however, death often came too quickly to capture the previously unphotographed subject while still alive. A few photographers and families compensated for this by posing their loved ones in positions that suggested life, such as opening the eyes or adding props to indicate sleeping.

The one pair of pre- and postmortem images known to exist illustrates the power of this juxtaposition of life and death. The caption for these images suggests one reason the formal pairing of Emmett Till's Christmas portraits and his dead body—a pairing that was repeated in the magazines and newspapers that reported on the funeral and trial—yields such affective power.

Burns's caption of the images *Premortem Daguerreotype of Boy Lying in Bed with a Ball* and *Postmortem Daguerreotype of the Same Boy Lying in Bed*, circa 1848, reads:

> The first, most unusual, image shows a sick boy in bed with a ball, which symbolized the joy of life in which he can no longer participate. . . .
> The second image shows the boy after he has died. . . . The spots on the boy's forehead indicate the development of a childhood exanthema, perhaps chicken pox or measles.[23]

Emmett's Christmas portrait has him posed with an object that represents a similar "joy of life"—a Philco television, which was by 1955 the American home's central vehicle of entertainment. However, his proprietary pose against the television as well as his stylish new outfit, a Christmas gift from his mother, depict a boy who has no idea that his death is imminent—less than nine months away. As one scholar said to Mamie Till, "That photo would come to define him for everyone. It would become so important in telling his story, starting at his funeral, where it had been on display in his casket. How ironic, [the scholar] noted, that the photo seemed to foreshadow something with such profound historical significance: the role that the media—especially television—would play in covering the civil rights struggle, a struggle that would intensify with the coverage of the murder trial."[24]

The spectacle of Till's body in the casket—the second image of this premortem/postmortem visual pairing—like the daguerreotype, shows not only the body but also the signs of its death. It is the visibility of the wound that compounds the affective power of the visual display. The fact that the mark of death on Till's body renders him nearly unrecognizable as human grants this generic dynamic much greater gravity.

The emotional power of the memento mori pictorial genre is premised upon making mortality both visible and meaningful. The genre originated in the seventeenth-century European still-life paintings known as *vanitas*. The genre was adapted to the photographic medium in the late nineteenth and early twentieth centuries. Because the images produced by photography are understood to offer documentary evidence of the physical existence of an actual body, the existential message of the memento mori—literally, "remember that you must die"—is explicitly linked to a real body—the subject of the memorial photograph. Barring witness of the actual circumstances of another's death—for instance, witnessing an act of murder—the spectacle of corporeal remains are understood by the viewer as proof of the cessation of life (death as an event) and as evidence of universal human vulnerability. It is the dead body made visible that unites in the mind of the viewer the abstract concepts of life and death via the notions of a humanity defined as such by its vulnerability.

The memorial photograph, therefore, both is and is not allegorical. Its use of allegory directs its viewer to what I am calling the *pedagogical imperative of death.* Its rhetorical strategy relies on the same consensual investment in the idea of a universal humanity that underwrites humane insight and is in part defined by mortality. The photographic medium demands that there actually be a body present in order for it to be represented in the memorial photograph. The mourning for or acceptance of one's own mortality that is the ambition of the memento mori is a visually prompted event—the spectacle of another's body after death. The self-conscious act of mourning, figured by the genre as psychologically productive and cathartic, depends upon the mistake embedded in humane insight—that one sees the dead body as (potentially) one's own. The endurance of the memento mori images demonstrates that the imaging of death and/or violence, and the spectator's humane insight that transforms these images into valuable lessons about human vulnerability, includes the most important lesson—how (not) to die.

In addition to the mourning that these images precipitate, these representations of the mortal body inform the viewer's knowledge of his or her own body's limits. Moreover, as Elizabeth Alexander argues, such images can illustrate the exceptional vulnerability of black bodies because they "suggest that 'experience' [the specific experiences of vulnerability known as pain and death] can be taken into the body via witnessing and recorded in muscle memory as knowledge."[25] Such knowledge may include race-specific knowledge of what spaces the black person can inhabit and transgress, and the limits of his behavior in those spaces.

Death, Derrida adds, is a teacher without peer in its ability to instruct the body and inform identity. "To live, by definition," he explains, "is not something one learns. Not from oneself, it is not learned from life, taught by life. Only from the other and by death. In any case from the other at the edge of life. And yet nothing is more necessary than this wisdom. It is ethics itself to learn to live."[26] The human project is not to learn to live, but to learn *how* to live—a query to which Derrida's simple reply is "justly." Derrida's reference to justice and his call that we heed the ghosts of the dead to develop "a *politics* of memory, of inheritance, and of generations" is echoed in Achille Mbembe's more pointed call for a "necropolitics" to eliminate "the state of exception" under which minority populations now live to render their "status of *living dead*" as well as the lives of those who have succumbed to death to crucially inform a just and equitable—in other words, a truly humane—way of living in the near future.[27] These amendments to the lessons of the dead—Derrida's assertion that the lesson is not merely a matter of individual self-preservation, but a broader project of ensuring individual and even global justice—describes the ideological alteration that Mamie Till made in making mourning a matter of public concern. With this recalibration, the lesson provided by Emmett Till's death was no longer how African Americans can avoid death at the hands of racist whites, but how all human beings can, in the name of justice, eradicate the racism that causes such deaths.

Mamie Till began this process of the radical recuperation of the dead black body from the debilitating logics of black submission and exceptional vulnerability by literally taking the body back from the hands of racist white officials. In her study of black death and funeral culture, Karla Holloway discusses the cultural importance of African American's tradition of reclaiming the bodies of dead kin. Holloway discovers that, in the heyday of the segregation era, Jim Crow regulations in the mortuary industry and the logistical necessity of consulting white undertakers "created an additional psychological burden for African Americans when death occurred in their community."

> White violence, including the vicious practice of lynching, was complicit in too many black deaths, and whites were often as disrespectful to black bodies in death as they were in life. . . . So, when black men embraced the burial business, they were responding not only to a business opportunity but also to a sense of cultural responsibility and community necessity. Black families *knew* black morticians—they were our kin, our neighbors, our fellow congregants in Sunday worship service.[28]

This insistence on placing the body of a deceased loved one in the care of another who would respect and, in two senses, properly preserve that body indicates, in its own way, a kind of justice through "just treatment"—exactly what that body was denied in life. The practice of reclaiming kin for burial preparation marks not only a final gesture of corporeal control—the body is wrested from those who might disrespect it—but also represents a practical maneuver. Through her many conversations with members of the funeral industry, Holloway discerns a pride in the skill of black undertakers and embalmers who, in their work on black bodies, are not only equipped to meet "the challenges of the varieties of skin tone among black folk but also . . . [can manage the] repair job that masks the residue of violent death."[29] These black undertakers are charged with making, and thought to be in a better position to make, the dead and maimed black body recognizable to the mourners as human and as kin.

Most significant to this discussion of looking and humane insight is how this racialized mortuary tradition also enables the mourner to take the visible body back by taking the body "in" through the act of sight. Much like the witnessing that "consolidate[s] group affiliations" through the spectacle of brutalized black bodies, this visual gesture of recognition affirms community and kinship bonds.[30] This gesture of "taking in" is aided substantially by the craft of black mortuary, by which I mean that industry's training in and objective of facilitating an open-casket funeral by rendering the body recognizable, looking as it had in life. This morbid realism enables the "final social encounter" to produce the empathy that results from the mourner's recognition of a shared humanity.

And yet it is precisely this refusal to acquiesce to "retouching"[31] the disfigured body—what amounts to the aesthetic realism of the mortuary industry—that made Emmett Till's funeral a political event and an activist gesture. I am arguing here that the funeral and mortuary industries have cultivated a form of realism that demands that one see the dead body either as it appeared in life or not at all (closed casket). Visually beholding and recognizing the body in this way is essential to the mourning process that has been codified by a North American funeral industry. By inversion, the Till funeral relied on the effects of this form of realism by presenting a body that seemed not to be what it was said to be.

An important facet to knowing that the body is properly cared for is the essential knowledge that the body has been buried and will stay buried, enduring no further insult and degradation at the hands of its enemies. What I am calling here *further insult* is what forensic pathologists refer to as *overkill*—the violent physical gestures (repeated stabbings, beatings, postmortem dismemberment) that visibly and metaphorically ornament the simple act of killing. To call those who defile a corpse "torturers" misses the point that the aggression is not about exerting power over a living body, but about performing a ritual demonstrating privilege over the dead body. In such instances, the extinguishing of life is not enough; the murder operates to kill not only the person, but the metaphysical bond—humanity—that connects him to his victim as well. Ashraf Rushdy explains this desire with respect to lynching, wherein it was understood that "the corpse was an object to be tortured, mutilated, collected, displayed. To snuff out life was rarely enough: more ritual was required."[32] Rushdy adds that "[e]ven a mob that had already hanged, maimed, and burned a man might still feel compelled to exhume his body in order to inflict further *indignities*."[33] The motivating threat here extends from the body's potential to signify as human even in death and inspires the ritualized act of stripping the body of its dignity.

In the Till funeral as in any funeral, the excessive violence of the murderers is countered by the mourners whose respect for the body and for the life it once contained acts as a sort of antidote to the previous acts of mistreatment. The act of mourning violent death operates in a figurative sense like the mortician's retouching, covering up the mistreatment of the body with its own articulate compassion. In its refusal to admit any covering up of the wounds or their source—racist violence—the Till funeral represents a radical departure from the standard. The mourner's compassion was not elicited through a visual presentation of the body as it appeared in life. On the contrary, it was elicited from mourners over and over again through the display of a body so unrecognizable that, as we have seen, even his mother admits to having initially had trouble recognizing it as the body of her son.

The mechanics of the act of mourning precipitated by visual confrontation is altogether thrown into question by the Till funeral. Although it can, with some certainty, be said that the effect of mourning (a product of empathy) is a consequence of the visual encounter with the actual body and not (only) its representation in photographs, the act of mourning is really encouraged by the guarantees offered by the funeral rituals themselves and, in this case, reinforced by mass media sources, including the mass-reproduced photographs, the captions of which declare that the body (re)presented in the coffin at the church altar is in fact the body that should be mourned.

The Mass Media Mourner

Other spectators besides Mamie Till and those present at the funeral were made mourners via mass media publication of the photograph. The publication and republication of photographs of Till's body in the black magazine *Jet* and the black newspaper *Chicago Defender* duplicated the mourner's viewing position. Perhaps more conspicuously than the lynching photographs of the *Without Sanctuary* exhibition that are discussed in the previous chapter, the pre- and postmortem photographs of Emmett Till position the photographs' viewers as spectators whose looks were politicized and empowered.

The seemingly passive occupation of looking was, in this visual scenario and at this historic moment in the history of African American civil rights, transformed into the empowered surveillance project of watching. We need not and, indeed, should not think of the image viewer as passive, but as

Boys Never Told Grandfather About 'Incident'

who escaped after the crime, told **JET**:

"When the men came, swearing and all, Grandma tried to awaken Bobo and hide him outside. But the men stormed in and told her to get back in bed and shut up before they beat 'hell' out of her.

"Grandma knew about the 'incident' because we'd told her and not Grandpa, who would have gotten angry at us. We'd gone into town Wednesday and were watching some boys playing checkers in front of the store. Somebody said there was 'a pretty lady' in the store and Bobo said he was going inside to buy some bubble gum.

"After a while, we went in and got Bobo but he stopped in the doorway and whistled at the lady. She got angry and followed us out, then ran toward a car. Some one hollered, 'She's getting a gun' and we ran."

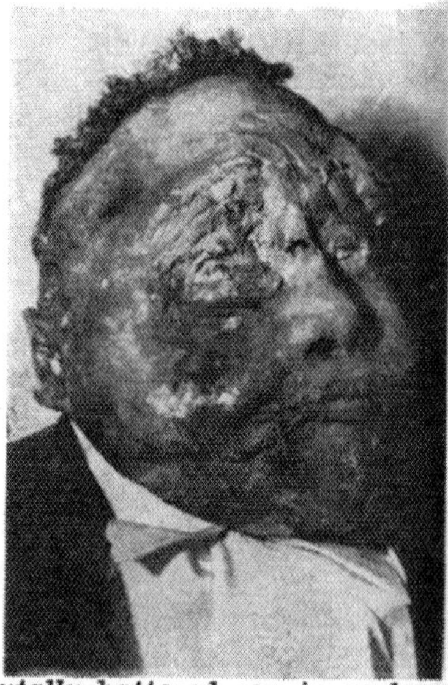

Mrs. Bradley got first look at brutally battered son in undertaker's morgue. More than 600,000, in an unending procession, later viewed body (r.).

Figures 7 and 8. *Jet* magazine photo spread on the murder of Emmett Till, September 15, 1955. Courtesy Johnson Publishing Company, LLC. All rights reserved.

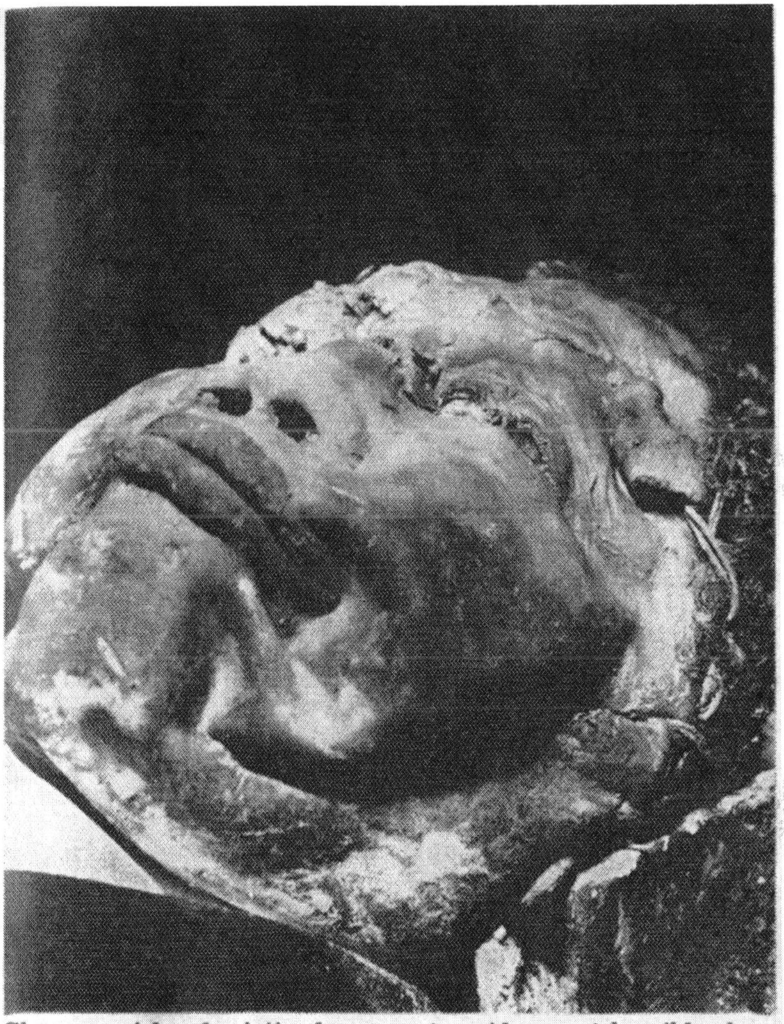

Close-up of lynch victim bares mute evidence of horrible slaying. Chicago undertaker A. A. Raynor said youth had not been castrated as was rumored. Mutilated face of victim was left unretouched by mortician at mother's request. She said she wanted "all the world" to witness the atrocity.

actively self-restraining. Recalling the repressive work of Emmett Till's uncle Moses Wright's self-restraint, we may understand watching to be motivated by an interest in self-preservation. We can, therefore, through this approach, come to appreciate differently the alternative activist solutions performed predominately by black women, and, specifically, black mothers, including Mamie Till, during the civil rights movement. The consequence is to call into question what Robin D. G. Kelley identifies as "the common claim that black mothers and grandmothers in the age of Jim Crow raised their boys to show deference to white people."[34] By understanding these women's instructions as preservationist acts of restraint, we can no longer accuse these women of "'emasculating' potential militants," but appreciate them as "arming their boys with a sophisticated understanding of the political and cultural terrain of struggle."[35]

Here, it seems necessary to discuss how the image of Till postmortem moved spectators to action.[36] It would seem that the distorted appearance of Emmett Till's body almost made its presence and its visual availability irrelevant for the purposes of public mourning. And yet the mourning for Till's body *is* augmented by its visual presentation. It was not newspaper articles and reporter monologues that caused people to faint or to fly into overwhelming expressions of grief. There is, without doubt, a difference between seeing a body and seeing a photograph of a body. Still, it may be that the very unreality of Till's corpse is what made the consequence of this specific act of mourning—political agitation—as reproducible as the photographic image of the body itself.

As several writers confess in their memoirs, a range of these sensations was elicited by the Till photographs. Muhammad Ali describes his encounter thus:

> A week after [Emmett Till] was murdered in Sunflower County, Mississippi, I stood on the corner with a gang of boys, looking at pictures of him in the black newspapers and magazines. In one, he was laughing and happy. In the other, his head was swollen and bashed in, his eyes bulging out of their sockets and his mouth twisted and broken. . . . I couldn't get Emmett out of my mind, until one evening I thought of a way to get back at white people for his death. . . . I remember a poster of a thin white man in striped pants and a top hat who pointed at us above the words UNCLE SAM WANTS YOU. We stopped and hurled stones at it, and then broke into the shoeshine boy's shed and stole two iron shoe rests and took them to the railroad track. . . . When a big blue diesel engine came around the bend, it hit the shoe rests and

> pushed them nearly thirty feet before one of the wheels locked and sprang from the track. . . . I'll never forget the eyes of the man in the poster, staring at us: UNCLE SAM WANTS YOU.[37]

The recollections of another athlete, Kareem Abdul-Jabbar, indicate a more subtle but similarly profound response to the postmortem photograph of Till: "I was eight years old when I saw a photo of Emmett's body in *Jet* magazine. It made me sick. His face was distorted, gruesomely bloated. I had no idea what happened to him, but my parents discussed it at length; and the *Jet* photo left an indelible image I could never forget. . . . The murder shocked me; I began thinking of myself as a black person for the first time, not just a person. . . . [A]ll of a sudden, the color of my skin represented danger."[38]

The memories of Abdul-Jabbar and Ali, not to mention those of other authors who cite the Till story in their memoirs, bespeak these authors' strong identification with the body represented in the pictures. The authors' narrations of their respective responses illustrate how "taking in" the picture of Till's brutalized body also meant "taking in" that which was not graphically represented in the photograph—a notion of systemic injustice that is determined by America's abiding racism. Through viewing the photograph, Abdul-Jabbar and Ali also "take back" their racially and sexually marked bodies by acknowledging and resisting the social parameters that have been placed on them. Their responses to this sentiment—Ali's railroad sabotage and Abdul-Jabbar's self-awareness that resulted in an altering of relationships with his white peers—in effect prevent the story of Till's murder from ending with the image of his tortured body, but give it the instructional edge that Derrida claims is integral to the relationship of the living to the dead. Ali and Abdul-Jabbar learn about death, specifically the death of a black male youth, and subsequently hold themselves responsible to the image.

The Courtroom Viewers

During the trial of his murder, Emmett Till's humanity was officially submitted to the work of justice and to the lens of humane insight. The pedagogical imperative of the image of mortality derives from an impulse for social justice, a desire to make death communicable (what Scarry calls "sharable"), and a desire to make the human being recognizable as a human being. This project of linking justice to a notion of humanity involves imbuing mourning with purpose, and granting the work of mourning a quantifiable goal. The goal—justice—is measured in terms of its responsibility to a notion of humanity that is operating both rhetorically (as bestowing the identity of humanity) and ideologically (as determining the discourse of justice itself). This dual invocation of humanity complicates things, to say the least. In one regard, as Derrida points out, humanity is "that unconditional dignity . . . that Kant placed higher, precisely, . . . than any economy, any compared or comparable value, any market price."[39] On the other hand, however, it also provides the terms in which human value is discussed. The confused version of humanity to which the pursuit of justice refers is both an item of (theoretical) exchange and the ideological criteria of the economy of exchange itself. The problem with this dually signifying humanity is that it threatens to invalidate the notion of justice altogether. In other words, the aim of justice is to quantify humanity, but the logic of humanity itself maintains that no single person's humanity is unequal to another's. Justice, in this case, can only perform two tasks: to serve as a superficial indicator of what is already known about the value of human life (that all lives are valued equally) or to provide a brazen violation of the essential tenets of humanity (that all human beings' lives are *not* valued equally in accordance with a notion of universal humanity). These competing definitions of justice and, by extension, of humanity are what are presented to the modern, state-sanctioned arbiter of value—the courtroom.

The prosecution in the case was charged with the task of proving not only Emmett Till's humanity and his attendant right to justice, but also that justice was being sought on behalf of the right body. In terms of the image, this meant making the image of Till's body recognizable on two fronts: as the body of Emmett Till and as the body of a human being. During the trial, Mamie Till's identification of the body and her assertion of recognition were called into question by the lawyers representing Till's alleged murderers. Mamie Till was asked not only to detail her method of recognizing the body received in Chicago, but also to repeat that act of recognition when presented with more photographs of the body to affirm that every photograph submitted into evidence indeed represented a likeness of her murdered child.[40]

The extent of the body's disfigurement—its unrecognizability as Emmett Till—was the basis for some testimony that no criminal act had been committed against the boy. One strategy in the defense attorneys' arsenal was to suggest that Till was still alive and well in Chicago and that the body found in the river had been deliberately planted. On the stand, Sheriff Strider suggested that the body found in the river could have been that of "a negro boy who disappeared over there at Lambert."[41] To cast upon the prosecution's narrative the shadow of doubt, the defense suggested in closing arguments that the National Association for the Advancement of Colored People (NAACP) and others had staged Till's death. A newspaper at the time reported this proposed sequence of events:

> J. W. Milam and Roy Bryant might . . . have abducted Emmett Till in the night. But if they did, they turned him loose three miles down the road at the Bryant store in Money and told him to walk home. Moses Wright had left his cabin, and driven down the road to Money and met Emmett coming home, and taken him to meet a friend from the National Assn. for the Advancement of Colored People, and the friend had persuaded Moses Wright to plant his nephew's ring on a "rotten, stinking corpse," which, when fished out of the river, would be identified by simple people as that of Emmett Till.[42]

Defense attorney John W. Whitten exploited this scenario and declared during closing arguments that "[t]here are people . . . who will go as far as necessary to commit any crime known to man to widen the gap between the white and colored people of the United States. . . . They would not be above putting a rotting, stinking body in the river in the hope it would be identified as Emmett Till."[43]

Because the defendants, Milam and Bryant, did not confess their crime before the court, the state was required to make its case using witness testimony and circumstantial evidence. And although the two photographs of Till's corpse that were admitted in the trial offered perhaps the most emotionally compelling testimony, they did not serve as incontrovertible evidence of his murder. The image of the mutilated body that was at the center of civil rights agitation in the public realm was radically stripped of any significance in the pursuit of justice in the Mississippi courtroom when the body depicted therein was decided to be unrecognizable as Till to any legally definitive degree. Paradoxically, the unrecognizability that conveyed such strong claims against racist brutality at the funeral in Chicago and that made it necessary for the spectator to give more than a glance in order to recognize the body as human was, in the courtroom, the grounds for excluding the image as evidence, for denying it so much as a glance, and for making the body and, by extension, the crime against that body invisible or, worse, not identifiable as a crime at all.

The ideas of photograph-as-documentary and the cachet of the photograph as unmediated visible proof were delegitimized in the courtroom by the legal requirements to prove the corpus delicti (the fact that a crime has been committed). The photographs themselves were not proof of murder. This missing equation—the crime as fact—prohibits the telling of the story of a crime that resulted in a death. It is a body that cannot be accounted for in language; it is an unnarrated body. The pedagogical imperative of the spectacle of death is deflected, and an anxious uncertainty takes its place. The absence of a narrative explaining the cause of death means that there is also no hope of learning how that death might have been avoided. Deprived of a material explanation for death, even an explanation as vague as "he was murdered," death has no lesson to teach the living. The memento mori is no longer a reminder; it is an image without affect.

The prosecution's failure to establish the corpus delicti was brought up by defense attorney J. J. Breland during his cross-examination of George Smith, sheriff of Leflore County. Breland used this point as grounds for objection, thereby preventing the witness from relaying Roy Bryant's confidential admission of guilt. When the court agreed to this point, the prosecution recalled undertaker Miller to the stand. The defense council continued to cast aspersions on the source of the wound above the body's right ear, suggesting that it may have been caused by "snag in the river." [44] But two days and four witnesses later, the presiding judge, Curtis Swango, had evidently been sufficiently assured that the death was due neither to natural causes nor to suicide and that the body was indeed that of Emmett Till. He overruled defense attorney Sidney Carlton's claims that the corpus delicti had still not been proven, and the trial was permitted to proceed.[45] The prosecution was therefore able to treat the case as though the crime that had been committed against Emmett was a given, and that their legal responsibility was to convince the court that the two defendants were in fact the perpetrators of the crime.

The prosecution also had to deflect the claims made by a series of witnesses for the defense that the body represented in the photograph was not the body found in the river. Although the body's extensive disfigurement (which both sides, defense and prosecution, concurred was likely the result of a severe beating) might have helped the prosecution's case by illustrating the extent of the brutality enacted upon it, it nevertheless had a detrimental effect on the prosecution's case because it permitted the defense to challenge the prosecution's claims that the body was indeed that of Emmett Till. More than likely this was the case, for why else would the prosecution insist on entering the postmortem photographs into evidence at all? The defense capitalized on this point when Sheriff Strider was called to the stand. According to the trial transcript, defense attorney John Whitten asked Strider if he "could . . . tell whether [the body] was a white person or a colored person?" to which Strider replied, "The only way you could tell it was a colored person—and I wouldn't swear to it then—was just his hair. And I have seen white people that have kinky hair," adding "if one of my own boys had been missing, I couldn't really say if it was my own son or not, or anybody else's. I couldn't tell that. All I could tell, it was a human being."[46] State attorney general Robert B. Smith presented Strider with a photograph during cross-examination and asked the witness "if that picture represents the condition of the body taken out of the river . . . ?" Strider confirmed that it did and added that "[a]t the time it was brought out of the water, [the body] was just as white as I am except for a few places around that was just a little darker than other places. And except for that, he was just as white as I am."[47]

A deconstructive assessment of how the photograph is ideologically figured here as a conveyer of unmediated truth reveals something that at first appears counterintuitive. In rejecting what the photograph represents—Emmett Till's body—Strider and other witnesses articulate a wholehearted belief in the photograph's ability to represent "a true likeness" of a body. But their denial and refusal to recognize the body represented in the photograph as the specific body of Emmett Till demonstrate the documentary limitations of photography; namely, that the photograph might not be able to represent sufficiently a body that is constantly evolving—aging, moving, dying, decomposing.

Even if Strider could not recognize the face in the photograph as that of Emmett Till, he could still, with some effort, recognize the face as that of a human being. As has been mentioned, proving Emmett Till's humanity was a key element to the prosecution's case, as it is to all civil rights cases. Yet throughout the investigation and the trial, the sheriff exhibited an undeniable disregard for black people's humanity, exhibited by his insistence on setting up a racially segregated area for the black reporters and his use of a racial slur as a solution to criticisms he received about his unpleasant demeanor.[48] It might therefore be reasonable and critically useful to claim that at least part of the reason Strider could not recognize the body in the photograph as the body of Till is because he could not recognize the body of Emmett Till, an African American boy that was represented in the photograph as the body of a human being in whose name justice could be sought. Strider could not extend humane insight to the image of a black person.

That Emmett Till's existence as a human being was not recognized by a prosegregationist racist is not in itself surprising. But as my own analysis and other critical work on the uses of lynching imagery have shown, the white supremacists' exhibition and circulation of visual documents of lynching (both photographs and actual body parts) are underwritten by and served (when they were produced) to reinforce a notion of a powerful and just white community. As discussed in the last chapter, it is not merely incidental, Shawn Michelle Smith suggests, that these images were often sent as postcards, a transmission so prevalent that it required legislation prohibiting it.[49]

The courtroom demands that Emmett Till be recognized as a justice-deserving human being represented a threat to this idealization of whiteness that claimed as a defining feature its special access to justice, which it both received and meted out. Oddly enough, Strider's own language betrays another oft-cited challenge to racial purity that racial supremacists usually reject. In his admission that the body at the river appeared to him as racially ambiguous, Strider spoke one of the truths of American racial heritage: that a history of miscegenation and racial "passing" has totally undermined any assertions of racial purity. Strider's statement that he has "seen a lot of white men with kinky hair" demonstrates not only his myopia in terms of racial critique, but also the parameters of a racially inflected notion of human beings.[50] That the body in the river was human he is certain; but that the body of Emmett Till—which Strider and the defense have, through a series of rhetorical gyrations, practically reasoned out of existence let alone sight—is human in any sense that he understands (that is, purely white and deserving of justice), he appears to have doubt.

Ultimately, the white jury permitted these doubts to free them from finding the defendants guilty.[51] It took them only sixty-seven minutes to acquit Milam and Bryant, and, as one juror famously remarked, it would have taken them less time had the jury reportedly not stopped for a drink of soda on the way back. It appears that the equation of whiteness and justice with the communal ties of race loyalty—both reducible to recognizing the white body exclusively as human and seeing humanity exclusively in whiteness—is an equation that foreclosed the possibility of Till's body ever being recognized either actually (in the postmortem photograph or the decomposed body itself) or discursively (in the language of justice). Quite literally over Till's dead body, the tribal bonds of Southern whiteness in the United States were strengthened. The acquittal also represented the reinforcement of what Sheriff Strider hoped would be forever preserved when he declared that "we haven't mixed so far down here and we don't intend to."[52]

Nevertheless, from that very moment, the way of life that Strider cherished would find itself strenuously challenged and legally dismantled. Yet in order for Sheriff Strider's cherished status quo to be preserved, the presumed impotence of the look must not be questioned by the spectator, but unconsciously accepted as a permanent given condition. Without a politicized notion of universal humanity to mediate one's view of a human corpse, one is ultimately not a mourner, but a voyeur. Neither of these is a particularly proactive position. The jury's failure to indict, compounded by the defendants' confessions in 1956—both events that underwent massive public exposure—only further insulted the peripheral onlookers' (that is, the mourners' and the voyeurs') relative impotence in the discursive realm of justice. To those onlookers who never believed in either the logic of segregation or in the logic invoked in the defense's case, the story's implausible conclusion—*not guilty*—mocked the powerlessness of the spectator and, moreover, reinscribed the alleged powerlessness of the look itself.

Instead of corroborating the juridical decision and the spectator's relative inability to effect narrative resolution, some onlookers of the Till case mobilized their role as onlookers into a political movement: the civil rights movement. This public recognized in the trial's resolution the inadequacy of the court's contribution to the conclusion of the murder narrative and, in so doing, challenged the privilege attributed to the American justice system, and the courtroom in particular, to determine a definitive conclusion.

4

Civil Rights and Battered Bodies

The civil rights movement of the 1960s was visually documented and circulated like no black movement before it, due in large part to the proliferation of televisual images. The abundance of images was also due to the conspicuous involvement of movement organizers in documenting and disseminating visual proof of their effort and their obstacles. Nonviolent campaigns such as the sit-ins, the freedom rides, and the march spotlighted the easy violence directed at lawful black citizens. Organizations such as the Student Nonviolent Coordinating Committee (SNCC), the Southern Christian Leadership Conference (SCLC), and the Congress of Racial Equality (CORE) not only recruited photographers and created their own media corps to take control of their wider representation but also engaged directly with journalists and orchestrated high-profile actions to ensure that their work in local southern American towns was exposed to national and international viewerships.[1]

The images of the violent confrontation between activists and opposition—the police and the anti-integrationist public—are documents of chaos in the face of black self-control. Pictures of solemn, well-dressed students engaged in study and joyful, singing marchers work with and against the footage and photos of bloodied faces and bitten limbs to produce a narrative of a banal black humanity interrupted by unwarranted and irrational violence.

The movement overall and these individual campaigns are themselves complex events, and there are a great many texts that discuss these in more detail than I am able to here. Rather than reproduce those studies, this chapter links the overarching goals of the civil rights movement to the enduring struggle for black humanity in America that has been discussed throughout this book. Here, I focus on the violence encountered during some of these nonviolent actions and unpack the aesthetics of their visual documentation in photographs and documentary footage. Taking to heart Sasha Torres's assertion that "black performances of physical suffering and political demand . . . [were both] a primary focus of the movement and a crucial key to its success,"[2] this chapter identifies the visual rhetoric used to invoke the injustice of black suffering as human suffering. The spectacle of African American suffering that had been repeatedly mobilized throughout the nation's history as outlined in previous chapters was again brought into high relief by the movement, this time by its utilization of nonviolent direct action as a means of "passive" protest.

As with the "passive" looking and mourning that I identified in the preceding chapter on the lynching of Emmett Till, here I challenge the characterization of the politically effective practice of nonviolent direct action as a passive process. It would seem that those who regard this strategy of civil engagement fail to fully appreciate the "directness" and "action" entailed in the strategy. By contrast, one of the strategy's most successful and prolific practitioners, Martin Luther King Jr., understood both the tactic and the circumstance in which it is expressed to be suffused with urgency. In "Letter from a Birmingham Jail," King explains, "Nonviolent direct action seeks *to create such a crisis and foster such a tension* that a community which has constantly refused to negotiate is *forced* to confront the issue. It seeks so to dramatize the issue that it can no longer be ignored."[3] Far from passive, the nonviolent direct actions that were the hallmark of civil rights resistance in the 1960s pushed segregation beyond its breaking point.

Images depicting the abuse of lunch-counter integrationists, mixed-race travelers, and peaceful black marchers met large audiences in public and in print. Indeed, the practice of passive nonresistance that characterizes the civil rights movement of the early 1960s was largely predicated on the visualization of news events that suffused the nation and the world by the mid-twentieth century. The movement's planned interventions allowed the nation, in particular the northern United States, and the world at large to see for the first time American racialized violence in the process of its unfolding. Televised new reports and the deliberate solicitation of coverage by civil rights organizations meant that the confrontations these interventions begat would be visually available to viewers very shortly after their occurrence.

The images produced during the Nashville sit-ins provide a clear example of how the spectacle of black-humanity-in-violation was produced and reproduced for a viewing public. The Nashville sit-ins of February 1960 followed in the footsteps of the sit-ins at the Woolworth's department store lunch counters in Greensboro, North Carolina, that had occurred earlier that month. With an awareness of the challenges faced by activists in that demonstration as well as in the sit-ins of the 1940s and 1950s sponsored by CORE and by the National Association for the Advancement of Colored People (NAACP), respectively, local Nashville students, many from historically black Fisk University and including student movement leaders John Lewis, Marion Barry, James Bevel, Bernard Lafayette, and Diane Nash, adhered to the principle of nonviolent direct action that characterized the earlier actions. Schooled in nonviolence by the Reverend James Lawson, a Vanderbilt divinity student who had spent ten years in India acquainting himself with Ghandian principles of nonviolence, the group of students, deliberately dressed in their Sunday best, "struck three major downtown five-and-tens" in downtown Nashville on February 13.[4] The sit-ins persisted in the following days, involving hundreds of students and expanding to other stores.[5] By February 27, not only local but national journalists had arrived to document the protest as well. At least one of these news organizations, the National Broadcasting Company (NBC), arrived with a film crew.

Months later, on December 20, 1960, NBC broadcast a special report on the sit-ins as part of its *White Paper* evening documentary series entitled "Sit-In." The report contained some of the starkest and now most recognized images of the protest itself. In her examination of "Sit-In," Sasha Torres concludes that the documentary developed and deployed particular techniques to appeal to its largest possible audience, one that included black viewers. These devices include the authoritarian narrator, the flashback, the vernacular black idiom, and the narrative "logic of inevitability"—the latter referring to the foreshadowing and leading that made the result of the sit-in to have been obvious if not preordained.[6] Torres's insights are very useful and offer a nuanced understanding of how the documentary functioned for the network that produced it and for the movement participants who adopted it as a training video. What Torres's discussion leaves out, though, is a close analysis of the footage of the original sit-in action and the graphic depictions of violence contained therein. An attention to the encounters and actions that actually appear in the sit-in footage is warranted, and I offer such an analysis here to enhance our understanding of how images of black embodiment in the face of violence have been central to the discourse of black humanity and liberation.

Although the documentary includes follow-up interviews and voice-over narration to present a fixed reading of the past, the footage of the sit-in itself shows the chaos of violence as it unfolded on that day.[7] A tightly framed close-up of and narration by sit-in Angeline Butler introduces the footage of violent confrontation at the lunch counter. The straight-on shot of Butler talking dissolves into a somewhat blurry profile shot of her, presumably filmed on what Butler terms the "first real day of violence"—February 27—that she is in the midst of discussing. The transition of Butler's narration from the diegetic interview to the nondiegetic voice-over narration configures the sit-in footage as a flashback that illustrates Butler's memory but also, according to Torres, implies a "logic of inevitability" that grants the documentary and its producers a narrative authority.[8] A series of profile shots of the other sit-in participants is shown, all while Butler narrates the day's sequence of events. These close-up profile shots are followed by progressively wider shots revealing multiple students—mostly black but also including white sit-in Paul Laprad—smiling and joking amiably while sitting at the lunch counter. The shots then widen further to reveal a crowd of young white men and police standing and strolling only a few feet behind and next to the students. With the film's visual revelation of these focused onlookers, the banality and bliss of the students at the counter is recontextualized and the suggestion of conflict is evident to the film's viewers for the first time. The appearance of this anti-integrationist constituency on screen authorizes the emergence of the voice of one of these men to interrupt Butler's narration and to offer, in a voice-over, his interpretation of the scene. With the man's concluding estimation that "[t]hey looked like they were just trying to egg on a fight," the film returns to a deep composition shot of three black sit-in participants, including Butler in the center, calmly minding their own business and exposing the man's characterization of their aggressiveness to be a lie. At this point in the film, Butler resumes the voice-over narration, and it is she whose head is shown, in a low-angle reverse three-quarter profile shot, before the next dramatic cut to the beating of the sit-in participants.

The beating is revealed from a high-angle medium shot that shows Laprad being pulled to the floor, surrounded by the feet of the anti-integrationist crowd. Now, for the first time in this film sequence, one hears what is presumably diegetic sound from the footage of the sit-in. The sounds consist of shouts from the crowd (one can faintly discern the cry, "Get him!") and the thumping of fists meeting flesh. Also for the first time the camera is revealed to be moving, retroactively figuring the preceding shots as establishing shots setting up for the "main event." The assault is thereby figured as the live, unmediated action that we viewers have been waiting to see.

The assault on the sit-in participants is the heart of the documentary, and its display is in a way the documentary's whole purpose. Not only does the assault fall near the midway point of the documentary—nineteen minutes into the documentary's fifty-six-minute run-time—but it satisfies the narrative buildup of the flashback portion introduced and framed by Butler's narration. The scenes of violence are not incidental to the film any more than they were incidental to the movement. Violent encounters between movement activists and opponents vividly translated the ideological conflict over civil rights to a pitched battle between the physical bodies of blacks and whites.[9] The footage of violence in the context of the narrative documentary is a dramaturgical decision that privileges the interaction of bodies precisely because of the roles that these bodies perform in the existential battle between good and evil. The value—to the viewer, to the documentary—of the assault on screen depends upon its presentation of carnal combat being legible as a dramatization of a divine battle between right and wrong.

Furthermore, the scenes of violence supply a sense of "live-ness" above and beyond that which the footage itself lends to the documentary. As Bernhard Giesen explains, "The exceptional nature of violence conveys a sense of utmost veracity and authenticity, it is grounded in a realm beyond volatile communication, fragile conventions, and faked pretentions: it has an absolute presence."[10] It is the violence depicted in the footage, not just the footage itself, that lends the documentary—more to the point, the movement *itself*—its authority as truthful and just. The "absolute presence" of violence in the narrative of the documentary, like the "absolute presence" of violence in the narrative of the movement, provides a harrowing and seeming incontrovertible testament to the right-ness of both of these pro–civil rights stories.

"Sit-In" makes the most of its footage of violence and offers dramatic shots of the abuse endured by activists. Laprad's beating is the first to be vividly displayed in the footage of the sit-in. From the camera's elevated view, the film shows members of the crowd winding up and delivering punches as Laprad huddles on the ground, shielding his head from the blows and scrambling to resume his seat. The documentary uses this opportunity to insert Butler's recollection of the moment and delivers her narration in voice-over as the slightly diminished sounds of the riot continue to play. Reinforcing the sense of live-ness to which the sit-in footage appeals, Butler states, "It seems to me that when it happened, that *all* of us wanted to be hit." With the utterance of the word *all*, the film reveals footage of black sit-in participants being assaulted at the counter, among them John Lewis, who darts across the counter in an attempt to escape the crowd's abuse.

The shot of the assault on the black students is short and in keeping with the aesthetic of documentary chaos that characterizes the other technically poor footage of the sit-in—blurry and oddly composed and comprised of rough edits. The camera moves, jerkily tracking the action as the crowd of white men lunge to grip students' coats, trying to pull them from their chairs onto the floor while the students, still with their backs facing the crowd, hunch and reach to grab hold of the counter to resist the men's force. The black student on the right of the screen succumbs to the violent tug and falls on the ground, below the counter and out of view. A rough edit progresses the action to the moment when Lewis vaults the counter, the neck of his jacket still in the grip of one of the men while his fellow sit-in is shown now standing but continually mauled by the crowd. Butler continues in voice-over: "This was an experience that we needed to keep our movement going and to keep ourselves going, and to convince ourselves that we really were nonviolent." The sequence ends with a cut to the students being led into the police wagon as the same roaring sounds of the riot play.

With the help of Butler's narration and the juxtaposition with calm establishing shots, the footage of black students being beaten resonates on screen as an image of black determination not trampled but augmented by the violence it received. This image of the stalwart black youth of America helped grant the movement the conviction and seriousness it sought to convey. The day after the broadcast, *New York Times* reviewer Jack Gould praised the report's ability to "capture the spontaneity of the events as they occurred in Nashville."[11] He went on to add that "primarily, the N.B.C. documentary was an immensely human account of the students at Fisk. Rarely has the screen shown a more attractive, intelligent, and determined group of youngsters who survived the trial of demonstrations and jail sentences without losing their sense of humor or naturalness."[12] Gould's comments do bear the patronizing language of someone thoroughly unaccustomed to seeing positive images of black people on screen, but it is prudent to dig deeper into his assessment as he is commenting on more than the revelation that good black people exist. As Torres explains, defaulting to a discourse of stereotype that simplistically pits positive representations against derogatory ones fails to account for the "subtle" and "insidious" expressions of blackness on view and risks "under-reading" the complexities of the programs that deploy and construct these images.[13] With this critique in mind, it appears more useful to interpret Gould's characterization of the sit-in participants as signaling their remarkableness as self-possessed youths who performed an outstanding respectability and bore the indignity of injustice right before our eyes.

Indeed, it was not only NBC and other print, television, and newsreel outlets that were responsible for the dramatizing of segregationist injustice during the sit-ins. The source of the image of movement activists' "moral authority," as Torres terms it, lay in the movement activists and organizers themselves. These activists and organizers were crucially involved in coordinating and choreographing their appearance on the stage of history.

The rubric determining the kind of movement—both physical and ideological—utilized in the movement actions was the tactic of nonviolent direct action. A delicately structured and frequently rehearsed balance of passivity and activity, nonviolent direct action defined the demonstrations of the early 1960s civil rights movement. We would do well to attend to the visual valence of the term *demonstration* here as it indicates the expectation of if not the need for an audience to bear witness to the event. As performance scholar Ron Eyerman explains, "demonstrations do not speak for themselves, they are performances which must be rehearsed and put in play, as well as seen and interpreted."[14] The movement necessarily recognized that there was a potential community of witnesses across the racial spectrum that would recognize the justice of the cause and the criminality of the violence that greeted them.

The movement's tactic of nonviolent direct action was crucial to dramatizing the pitched battle for racial justice in America. As in the prior struggles for black liberation discussed in this book, the civil rights movement framed its pursuit of earthly justice for black people in spiritual terms. The strategy of nonviolent direct action called upon activists' faith and onlookers' emotions to effect a spiritual and emotional change in not just law but also attitude. Yet again, the humanity of black people was linked to the humanity of the wider nation. Martin Luther King Jr., one of the best and most prolific articulators of the movement's use of nonviolent direct action, explained the connection between faith and humanity thus: "The nonviolent resister has faith in the future. He somehow believes that the universe is on the side of justice. So he goes about his way, struggling for man's humanity to man, struggling for justice, for the triumph of love, because of this faith in the future and this assurance that he has cosmic companionship as he struggles."[15] King's statement refers to a concept of universal humanity, one that is "cosmically" inevitable and accessed and activated by the nonempirical—faith. In this statement and elsewhere King defines humanity as itself an act of faith. As such, however, humanity for King does not have an uncertain future; to the contrary, justice is asserted as an absolute Truth, an inevitable destination for a global narrative that, to paraphrase King's famous citation, invariably "bends toward justice."[16]

King was certainly not alone in conceiving of justice in terms of universal humanity. The demand for freedom that emblazoned the banners of the 1963 Birmingham children's march ("Freedom now!"), that was described as the objective of the 1961 to 1965 integrationist bus riders ("freedom rides"), and that lent its name to the summer 1964 voter registration campaign ("freedom summer") called out specific, current injustices—segregation and voting restrictions—while asserting its objectives—integration and voting rights—in universalist terms. The call for freedom identified the invalidity of "separate but equal" and made equality among human beings, across races, a project of spiritual and legal liberation. Freedom's sister cry, "We shall overcome," was the slogan culled from a pro-union song that pointed even more explicitly to the arc of justice—the higher plane of justice and humanity—that movement activists were compelled to pursue, realities of racist policies and attitudes be damned.

The discourse of universal rights and freedom for all expressed by King, the freedom riders, SNCC, and others also pointed to the lie of current invocations of universal humanity espoused by a postwar America enamored with the vision of an equally accessed American Dream. Movement rhetoric checked the national self-regard as "the land of the free" by vividly illustrating the systematic repression of a full 10 percent of the US population.[17] The movement demonstrated that bravery in protection of this ideal of freedom was as much if not more often to be found in the young activists who were not afraid of challenging the status quo.

The bodies of protestors vivified a competing narrative for social justice, one in which radical changes in local customs and federal interventions were made possible and were likely outcomes. The movement capitalized on the image of bodies acting and literally *moving*—sitting, riding, marching—to bring about change. Both the goal and the strategy of the movement were to reform how black bodies could inhabit spaces. Consequently, the movement capitalized on the depiction of the black body as fully human bodies, not only rights-bearing but also entitled to the joys of unencumbered physical expression. Black bodies and the bodies of sympathetic whites literally moved in the civil rights protests into the streets and then into the jails to express their desired freedom and to expose the illegitimacy of the forces that currently restrained them. Conversely, the curtailing of movement protests by civilians and police were explicitly shown to be violating the American principles and civil protection of the rights to free assembly and free speech, exposing an untenable failure of the American way that was especially fetishized during the era of the Cold War.

During a period of retrenchment after the sit-ins in which the large-scale ambitions of SNCC were decided, SNCC coordinator Ella Baker pressed for the deliberate exclusion of the press so as to permit the movement's "unspoiled birth."[18] Nevertheless, the tactic of demonstrating injustice inevitably led to a mass-media-supported publication of the movement activism. Indeed, sit-in participant Bernard Lafayette was cognizant from the start of the need for a great quantity of onlookers beyond just those who were immediately present and therefore "took time to talk to people in the media," which was seen to have "a very important role; a necessary role."[19]

The movement recognized that the visual field was a site of battle. Various movement organizations solicited the work of photographs and established media corps to take some control of their public visual representation.[20] Underscoring the volatility of the image was the violence directed at the image makers themselves and at the tools of image production. The vicious attack on black reporter L. Alex Wilson, an editor at the Memphis *Tri-State Defender*, during the integration of the Little Rock, Arkansas, high school was one of these. In photographs printed in the *New York Times*, the *Los Angeles Times*, and elsewhere across the nation, Wilson is shown being kicked, pushed, and gripped in a headlock. So powerful and so legible were the images of the white mob's assault on Wilson, the *New York Times* used one of these rather an image of the black students on its front page on May 24, 1957, to illustrate the racial strife being enacted in Little Rock.

The Associated Press (AP) photograph that the *Times* used is horrifying in its dynamism. In the image, Wilson is seen kneeling on the grass, holding a hat in his right hand, with his head bowed and directly in the line of his attacker's upward-thrust shoe that hovers only inches from Wilson's face. While the crowd of onlookers seems to stand still in the background, the body of the white man assaulting Wilson is shown in the middle of his violent gesture of kicking Wilson in the head. The attacker's gesture is so dynamic and so precarious that it is instantly recognizable as a movement rather than a pose. Indeed, there is no way that the attacker could hold this position, balanced on his right foot, his torso leaning to the right in an incline that defies gravity and would only be counterbalanced by the kicking movement of his levitated left leg. The photograph operates, therefore, like a movie still or a photo decontextualized and edited out of Eadweard Muybridge's locomotion studies—as an image whose work is not to offer a complete depiction of

Figure 9. Reporter Alex Wilson attacked in Little Rock, Arkansas. Will Counts Collection: Indiana University Archives (P0026619).

movement but to gesture to the inexorable movement that lies beyond this particular image.

As such, the image of Wilson's assault reveals not merely violence, but also, importantly, violence in action—a kinetic violence in which the newspaper viewer cannot intervene. The AP image of Wilson's abuse, complete with motion blurs and awkward composition, contains what Sasha Torres identifies as "the formal [visual] markers of the political process that is unraveling before our eyes: the loss of the camera's control of the image is one of the things that tells the audience that political control, too, is up for grabs."[21] The viewer is thereby confronted with a story that is in the process of unfolding. Although the specific moment depicted in the photograph of Wilson is over by the time it has been printed and circulated, the narrative of racial strife that the *Times* sought to illustrate with this image is still ongoing by the time of its printed appearance the morning after the attack. The discourse of the newspaper as the never-ending tale of current events consequently figured the violence in Little Rock and against integration more generally as potentially a violence without end.

Rejecting, as do I, Susan Sontag's too-easy dismissal of images of violence as exploitative and ethically inert,[22] media scholar Susan Sliwinski turns to the insight offered in Virginia Woolf's *Three Guineas* (1937) for testimony on the violent image's real power. Reading Woolf's discussion of the Spanish War photographs that appeared in Woolf's morning paper, Sliwinski makes sense of what could be termed, borrowing the language of Benedict Anderson, an imagined community of humanity produced by viewing the images of atrocity in the mass media format. What looking at the images alongside an imagined community of fellow onlookers offers to the world is an identification of what constitutes the unacceptable treatment of a human being, starting with an identification of the unacceptable treatment of *this* human being depicted here. Moving from the reaction of one onlooker to envisioning the reaction of a community of onlookers "demonstrates the 'moral character' of humanity."[23] If images of the suffering of others provoke outrage, they do so because they inspire the very language and values of human rights that the image viewer sees being violated. As Sliwinski explains, "In this respect, distant observers become the heralds of the ideals of human rights because they alone are in a position to proclaim that which belongs to the common human understanding."[24]

Benedict Anderson's abiding great insight has been the virtual consolidation of nationalist thought via what he calls "national print-languages," a wedding of the popular vernacular and nationalist thought underwritten by "print-capitalism."[25] The national newspaper is an archetype of this enterprise in its construction of communities that cohere across time and space through print and the readers' imaginations. As Anderson explains, "[T]he very conception of the newspaper implies the refraction of even 'world events' into a specific imagined world of vernacular readers . . . [who also share] an idea of steady, solid simultaneity through time."[26] We should bear in mind that newspapers and other mass media outlets can construct other communities, not just ones that cohere to national boundaries. Indeed, the newspaper and televisual coverage of the civil rights movement established, in large part due to the emotional appeal of the images of violence and dignified black suffering, a widespread moral community that rendered segregationist appeals to racism and tradition publically unacceptable. With the segregationists' attacks on press image makers themselves, the aims of the civil rights movement and the free press could only appear to be morally aligned.

In fact, the violence encountered during the integrationist freedom ride campaign was so equally distributed between the press and the freedom riders themselves that media outlets saw no choice but to include themselves in their stories. The press corps that prepared to meet freedom riders as they arrived in Montgomery, Alabama, on May 20, 1961, were subjected to assaults by a prosegregation mob that had gathered at the bus station. The injuries sustained by the reporters were nowhere near as horrible as those endured by the freedom riders themselves, among them Jim Zwerg and John Lewis. A shocking photograph of the pair, showing Lewis's bloodstained shirt and Zwerg probing his mouth for missing teeth, would appear in newspapers and photo magazines nationwide. *Life* paired another image of the wounded Zwerg and images of the burning freedom rider bus in Anniston, Alabama, with blurry, clandestine photographs of NBC cameraman Maurice Levy being kicked and a portrait of *Life*'s own reporter Don Uhrbrock seated next to the photographer of Levy's assault, a battered and bloody Norman Ritter.[27]

These assaults on white members of the press and other white activists dramatized the underlying fear of white American society as well as the overarching message of the pro-black movement: that no one is safe when white supremacy fights to survive.[28] In the demonstrations and photographs in which black and white, activist and bystander, are shown to be equal recipients of violence, the case for universal humanity is made clear through the equitable spilling of blood by both races. In the Montgomery riot, race and rank did not matter, nor did an official edict of protection from the US president John Kennedy and the US attorney general Robert Kennedy. Though the freedom ride had proceeded to Montgomery based on verbal assurances offered by Alabama governor John Patterson, the violence that subsequently met the riders demonstrated just how exposed law-abiding, nonviolent citizens were to the ultimate degradation of their right to bodily integrity.[29]

The cameras of photojournalists and others affiliated with movement organizations did more than expose violence after the fact. Often enough, the cameras actually made movement possible because "[t]heir presence afforded movement workers a measure of protection against their segregationist opposition by signaling the capacity to broadcast southern race trouble nationally."[30] Much like today's society of surveillance in which police brutalities and other violent engagements are captured and uploaded by a citizenry armed with mobile cameras and the means to distribute their images, prosegregationist societies understood that the scope of their violence would have to be restrained when the cameras were out and the lights were up. Consequently, the eruptions of violence during the middle of the day and in very public areas galled many media onlookers who could read the counterprotestors' aggressive actions as grossly defiant of their own visual interventions into the scenes.

Both national media outlets and civil rights activists alike played important parts in the unfolding drama of the civil rights revolution. But for that drama to reach its satisfying end and for the revolution to truly take hold, a significant number of onlookers needed to be moved. As one scholar explains, "Social movement is a form of acting in public, a political performance which involves representation in dramatic form, as movements engage emotions inside and outside their bounds attempting to communicate their message. Such performance is always public, as it requires an audience which is addressed and must be moved."[31] Images—in particular photographic and motion picture images—are documents that can move spectators as a collectivity, a "virtual collectivity . . . where the ideal of a shared humanity literally comes into view."[32] The act of looking thereby becomes its own kind of movement, a movement toward justice through the spectacle of injustice.

If the prosegregationist southern population did not necessarily appreciate the power of published images of assaults on protestors, the prosegregationist press did. Southern newspapers that were opposed to the movement's aims understood the power of the image to sway viewers and consequently refrained from publishing images of the protests. Instead, they buried the stories on inner pages of their publications and refrained from publishing photographs of the conflict. One study of the two prosegregation Birmingham newspapers discovered that "[t]he use of photographs appears to have been highly selective. . . . Neither paper used any of the famous shots of the use of police dogs or hoses that were used around the world. In the later stages, the [Birmingham] *News* printed many photographs, but they do not show Negroes knocked down by hoses or with clothing ripped by dogs."[33] These same scenes would prove "irresistible" to other, nonlocal press constituencies and found their way into national newspaper and television reports.[34] According to former SNCC photographer Danny Lyon, by the time of the Birmingham riots in May 1963, "[t]wo-and-a-half years after it had begun in earnest, the civil rights movement was finally discovered by the American media. It was a front-page story and would remain so until displaced by Vietnam."[35]

The images of police brutality—brutality that was sanctioned by then governor Eugene "Bull" Connor and unleashed upon the young black marchers during the Birmingham protest—have rightfully been cited as important to the successful passage of many civil rights laws. Part of the success was due no doubt to mass media's implicit and sometimes explicit framing of the civil rights struggle as a righteous battle against the evil of segregation. As Martin Berger notes, "[W]hite media outlets in the North published photographs throughout the 1960s that reduced the complex social dynamics of the civil rights movement to easily digested narratives, prominent among them white-on-black violence."[36] According to Berger, the images of black protesters enduring violence at the hands of white officials and civilians diminished the authority of the abused black body by reinscribing it into a familiar narrative of black victimization and white power. The evidence provided in this book demonstrates that the civil rights movement was not the only nor indeed the first pro-black movement in the United States to mobilize the image of the wounded black body. We should be cautious of conflating "wounded" with "victim" here, however. Such slippage ignores that the agitations that utilized the wounded black body were intended to point out in stark visual terms the injustice of black victimization. The image of black suffering served to signal the depravity and immorality of white citizens, national character, and state law. Berger misses the point somewhat in asserting that the images of black abuse during the passive resistance interventions of the civil rights movement only provided a spectacle of black victimhood. Rather, the images and performances illustrated black potency as self-restraint in the face of violent white gyrations meant to cover a lack of self-control. Indeed, the tactic of nonviolent direct action was premised upon the power of suffering to convey an image of black inner peace and divine conviction.

Berger is correct in pointing out, though, that the stakes of this visual campaign were not just the victory of the civil rights movement but also, importantly, the actual bodies that were battered and bloodied in the movement's aim. The ironic aims of the destruction of physical bodies in search of a higher goal are discussed further in the conclusion where we necessarily reflect on the cost paid by black and white individuals in service to a wider struggle. But what Berger's critique misses overall is that black organizers, not white media outlets, were fully aware that their interventions might lead to scenes of violence. This assertion is not a repetition of the prosegregationist line of the day that blamed integration activists for bringing violence with them. Integration activists were not unwitting victims or belligerents who "had it coming." We can make a more subtle and powerful point about black agency and embodiment by attending to the sophisticated intellectual work entailed in effectively staging a protest.

The oft-cited John F. Kennedy declaration that Eugene "Bull" Connor "had done more for civil rights than almost anybody else"[37] should not be given the authority of a fair assessment of the civil rights movement. Privileging white racists such as Connor and the counterprotest mobs irresponsibly renders the incredible commitment, fortitude, and especially the *actions* of the activists as mere catalysts for a white master narrative of the nation's struggle over civil rights. To ignore the actions and the suffering of those who put their lives on the line is itself an act of extreme omission and veers stunningly close to bigotry itself.

The violence enacted on black and white activist bodies throughout the civil rights movement era moved sympathetic spectators because these well-planned demonstrations of antisegregationist conviction and black humanity—here aligned with respectability and signaled by physical appearance, intellectual competence, and youthful innocence—were forcibly interrupted by the violence of countermeasures. As Columbia Broadcast System (CBS) reporter Eric Sevareid commented in 1963, "A newspaper or television picture of a snarling police dog set upon a human being is recorded in the permanent photoelectric file of every human brain."[38] The violence enacted registered as unwarranted and unsolicited and was indelibly equated with injustice. Movement demonstrations exhibited protestors embodying an ideal humanity characterized by self-possession, compassion, and even joy while opponents and law enforcement demonstrated the worst—brutality, a lack of compassion, and a lack of self-control. The images of the civil rights movement illustrate a black-authored narrative of self-determination and autonomy—in short, a version of black humanity premised upon power and agency—that superseded and even confounded the conventional mainstream narrative of blackness in America.

5

A Litany for New Orleans, 2005

For those of us who live at the shoreline
standing upon the constant edges of decision
crucial and alone
—Audre Lorde, "A Litany for Survival"

This book ends in the place it began—New Orleans.

In 2005 New Orleans supplied newer, haunting images of black bodies in pain and in death after Hurricane Katrina. The category 5 storm that made landfall on August 29 tested and breached the inadequate infrastructure and institutional ineptitude that would elicit shock and criticism from Gulf Coast residents and the world at large. In the days, weeks, and months that followed the city's flooding, the world saw numerous corpses—under a shroud behind the Superdome and floating in the streets turned rivers—mostly via the mass media (newspaper, magazine, television, and Internet) outlets. The appearance of these images, amid an otherwise "tightly controlled visual landscape" that included a marked absence of Iraq war dead, a "set of troubling visual representations . . . emerged that both shocked and shamed the nation."[1] The Federal Emergency Management Agency (FEMA), aware of the damage that pictures of the post-Katrina disaster would do to their own image as sympathetic rescuers, prohibited journalists from accompanying their official rescue missions in hopes of preventing mass media distribution of photographs of the dead. Opposing image-making with action—an opposition that over the course of this book I have attempted to reveal as false—New Orleans mayor Ray Nagin furiously declared, "I don't want to see anybody do anymore goddamn press conferences. Put a moratorium on press conferences. Don't do another press conference until the resources are in this city."[2] Once again, the image of the black dead was a site of struggle.

It is a small sign of victory for black humanity that the image of its defilement could register the obscene failings of federal and local authorities. The

Figure 10. The body of a victim of Hurricane Katrina. Getty Images/AFP/James Nielsen.

stark spectacles of abandoned black folks signaling for help on rooftops and pathetically shrouded with discarded bedsheets in death certainly did entail vibrant discussions about a wide range of structural inequities in which race and class were the common denominator. Nagin's radio interview, however, indirectly addresses the other, less radical purposes to which the image of black suffering are put when they are conscripted into an official narrative of rescue and resurrection.

Official and corporate media outlets package scenes of atrocity to abet readings that condemn nature or the victims themselves for the tragedy. African American visual scholar bell hooks calls out the brutal truth of our contemporary mass media moment in which there is "no 'perceived market' for" antistereotypical counterimages of African Americans. Unlike the era of the civil rights movement, "the erosion of oppositional black subcultures (many of which have been destroyed in the desegregation process) has deprived us of those sites of radical resistance where we have had primary control over representations."[3] When considering the publications of current mass media, which are notably reticent to bring race critiques to the forefront of their analysis, we would do well to address "the interaction between visual culture and the practice of democracy [in terms of] the ways and the means by which our popular aesthetic forms frame, address, and resolve the expectations of the audience."[4] In the case of Katrina, images have been used to illustrate narratives of powerful natural forces and poor black residents' willful disregard of evacuation orders. These narratives omit and leave unseen the impact of wetland devastation due to contracts with private companies, massive governmental mismanagement and disregard, and the logistical failure of canceling public transportation services despite a significant population with no recourse to private vehicles.[5] The contextual tidying of the image threatens to undo the populist and democratic aims of photojournalistic image.

These narratives of disaster, accompanied by illustrative images of devastation, have privileged corporate relief agencies such as the Red Cross in favor of more effective local and grassroots organizations that draw upon the expertise of local residents and organizations and that are better able to respond to the specific needs of local communities.[6] "Activist tourism" has been another consequence of these narratives that recommend, regardless of evidence to the contrary, that all volunteering results in a positive outcome. This model has produced an influx of uninformed aid workers. Their imported solutions are often a poor fit in communities and, worse, inspire resentment when they ignore those communities' own activist networks.[7]

Such tourists and liberal organizations are responding in part to images of black suffering that have been construed as black obstinacy and incapability. Unlike previous instances of black embattlement discussed in the preceding chapters, mainstream discourse for the most part did not link the disastrous fallout of Katrina to underlying structural problems of racism and poverty that would have indicted biased policies and institutions. Instead, much of the discourse blamed the victims and survivors themselves. An examination of mass media coverage of Katrina revealed a reliance upon the rhetoric of "presupposition to construct victims and survivors as irresponsible."[8] Such coverage "encourage[d] readers to make an implicit value judgment about victims' and survivors' (ir)responsibility" and confronted readers with the question, "If they put themselves in this position, why should we help them?"[9] One way to resolve this question is to figure those affected as needing not only help rebuilding but education in basic priorities as well. In this case, the visibility of suffering did not expose the external sources of that pain; rather, the examination of the image ended with the image itself, and the pained bodies themselves were held responsible for their condition.

Blaming the corporal bodies of human beings rather than the corporate bodies of government and private institutions is a trend in recent political discourse. (One can think there of the appeal of one of Mitt Romney's 2012 presidential slogans—"We Built It"—that emphasized individual achievements as it deemphasized and critiqued various forms of government assistance.) Since the rise of an ossified version of American patriotism in the wake of the attacks of September 11, 2001, and a contraction of America's discourse on humanity, images of black suffering have not substantially interrupted the national self-perception as a society fully committed to its citizens' human rights.[10] In the case of Katrina, those black people who were capable of resisting the assumption of their image into a narrative of recovery risked relegation to "familiar stereotype[s] about black criminality"[11] that undermined their strident critiques of government failings. For those onlookers like scholar Joy James who remain committed to African American social welfare, "It was not human suffering per se, but suffering accompanied by repression embedded in the injunction of death for the resourceful who didn't want to roll or rot in misery that radicalized [her and others] into seeking more voices" that countered the oft-expressed view that havoc and barbarism were the inevitable outcomes of blacks thrown into survivalist mode.[12]

The victims of Katrina who acted on the part of their own survival were, in the eyes of the mass media and their public, altogether too capable to merit the status of "victim." If anything, the Katrina survivors were victims of their own industry whose quite logical work toward diminishing their experience and, consequently, their appearance of vulnerability actually mitigated their recognition as victims. In other words, by acting autonomously to rescue themselves from death through acts designated as "looting" by the Associated Press,[13] the survivors were unwittingly appealing to another racially coded image—that black people are dangerous and to be feared.

The only people who were allowed unquestionably to claim and to maintain victim status were the dead. It is here, again, that we are confronted with the untenable price of the black body's recognition as human. The criteria for being spoken of as human is that one must only and always be spoken *for*, incapable in death to speak one's own suffering. Although the living Katrina victims' states of abandonment and deprivation explicitly indicated their vulnerability, it was those who were conquered by vulnerability—the dead—who were clearly recognizable as vulnerable, even though they were most certainly not in a position to themselves appreciate this recognition of their humanity. If spared the designation of being too stubborn to leave, the dead of Katrina were fixed—like the photographic object—in a state of victimhood by their deaths. This fixing made it possible to accept the dead black bodies as nonthreatening images. And indeed, neighboring townspeople admitted that they would rather contribute to the post-Katrina effort by hosting dead black people than by housing living black people. Entry into the status of the preferred dead was articulated as a literal welcome by at least one neighboring resident whose town was used to house the Katrina dead; said St. Gabriel resident Theresa Roy, "I'd rather have them here dead than alive. And at least they're not robbing you and you [don't] have to worry about feeding them."[14]

Shortly after a basic infrastructure was established in New Orleans, less recovered parts of the city were made into tourist destinations. Today, a century and a half after the Lalaurie affair produced its morbid exhibition of suffering black bodies, there are other gruesome displays available for spectatorial consumption in New Orleans. These tours package "black New Orleans" for predominantly white, monied visitors who are paraded before scenes of destruction that are accompanied by a script that "at its dubious best casts black people as victims, and at its worst elides the issue of race altogether."[15] One tourism company, Gray Line Tours, currently offers on its website a special "Hurricane Katrina" tour of New Orleans during which, the company's website states, visitors can "[d]rive past an actual levee that 'breached' and see the resulting devastation that displaced hundreds of thousands of U.S. residents." At one time, the website also advertised a "Souvenir Hurricane Katrina book available for purchase at departure point!" that enables tourists to fetishize the image of destruction while they contribute further to the tourism companies' profits.[16]

Indeed, the aftermath of Katrina is interesting with respect to tourism, precisely because of how it makes parts of New Orleans simultaneously invisible and hypervisible—a paradox not unfamiliar to black Americans. The authors of the essay "To Render Ourselves Visible: Women of Color Organizing and Hurricane Katrina" in the South End Press Collective's powerful anthology *What Lies Beneath: Katrina, Race, and the State of the Nation* (2007) make the stakes of this dynamic clear. Their succinct explanation merits quotation in length.

> Oppressors render the oppressed invisible or hypervisible relative to how the situation benefits their agenda. Invisibility can be used as a tool of oppression, because if a people can't be seen, then their work can be discounted, their experience of violence and oppression can go without recourse, and their lives can be devalued. Hypervisibility, on the other hand, can be used to stigmatize people or to easily identify them as an object of fear or a target for violence.[17]

Fixed by the gaze that fetishizes black criminality and victimization and offered nary a glance at black self-determination and resilience, the black working class of New Orleans and the Gulf have found little actual help in the image. With outsiders determining the gaze, those areas and people who were normally not pictured would come, during the crisis, to be intensely photographed and scrutinized, and areas that were formerly off-limits became primary destinations for both press corps and tourists.

Outsiders turning to New Orleans, be it for philanthropy, pleasure, or profit, are capitalizing on the image of New Orleans's black presence even as the city's black residents turned refugees face obstacles to return to and restart their communities. The image of New Orleans and of the Gulf Coast as crucially influenced by a historical and continuing black presence suffers from the strangled mortality that images, in particular photographic images, create. Roland Barthes outlines the fatalist impulse of photography: to commemorate in the present a moment and environment and even persons that will inevitably pass from view over time, their demise memorialized but also predicted by the image produced. Obsessed with the moment in time, the photographic image "produces Death while trying to preserve life."[18] Looking at Katrina-ravaged New Orleans, we detect the insufficiency of the image that is passed off as a solution in itself. As performance scholar Peggy Phelan explains, "Our encounter with the photograph always occurs after the event recorded within it. The belatedness of photography reminds us of our tendency to arrive too late and perhaps especially to arrive too late to appreciate the unique drama of our mortality."[19] Uncannily enough, the tragedy of post-Katrina New Orleans can be regarded as itself due to the "too late" arrival of relief aid along with a failure of foresight in levee engineering. Several arrivals of interested outsiders and few returns of actual residents have rendered much of the region but a spectacle of its past. With black suffering and death relegated to inert images, other interests are able to capitalize on loss.

Conclusion

This study's return to New Orleans to look at and discuss images of the region's residents in the immediate wake of Katrina occasions an opportunity to activate the image by addressing what, or better, *who* has been haunting this book's examination of black death and suffering—those black people whose images founded a rhetoric of black humanity and American justice.

Images of black suffering and death seem to have signified most powerfully and fruitfully for the symbolic of black humanity and the protection of black dignity when the image points to the threat of a broader demise—the demise of humanity as a whole. It is when the nation was pointed at the abyss, the trajectory of America's Great Experiment in uncertain hands, that the recognition and salvation of black humanity promised to restore the humanity of the nation as a whole. The success is bittersweet; although the strategy succeeds in bringing those in power around to protecting black humanity, the value of black humanity itself and the awful loss that is the death of a black person is mitigated as though the loss of black humanity is not enough in itself to mourn. We now view the victories of the black liberation movements that made use of the image of its dead and its pained as crucial if not inevitable parts of the national press toward justice. But with slavery, lynching, and Jim Crow firmly relegated to the so-called wrong side of history, abiding and renewed violence against black people is disregarded as anomalous and irrelevant, illegible in the script of an exceptionalist national discourse that regards itself as the sole arbiter of justice and identifies as terrorist any who claim it in their own, competing name.

Rarely in recent years do images of black suffering interrupt the discourse of a tightly controlled media landscape. As one writer bemoans, "There was a time when the water from hoses punished the bodies of men, women, and children standing up for what they believed in, and the news came and shamed the nation into action. Now the news comes and governmental onlookers have counterprogramming to tell you that what you have just witnessed was just a figment of your imagination or liberal bias."[20] In the face of a powerful corporate media landscape, it is imperative that now more than ever not only that images of black people and black life—including black death—appear but also that those images are controlled—produced, reproduced, contextualized, and published—by black people themselves. Frequently, however, images of tragedy are figured as stony memorials, called upon only to bear silent witness to unheeded lessons. The resistance to reading Katrina for the lessons it offered to teach us about the value of black life is made clear by one resident who "[y]ear after year . . . watched the anniversary for Katrina pass while people gathered around flagpoles two weeks later to mourn the deaths from 9/11."[21]

Perhaps the political and ethical force of the images of black suffering that emerged from Katrina were diluted by the incorporation of the civil rights movement of the 1960s into a national master narrative of democracy or by the retrenchment of ideas of black wantonness and criminality publicized in the 1980s and '90s with images of Willie Horton and welfare queens. Perhaps many of us never saw black suffering for what it was at all, our vision restricted by a “force of antiblackness” that “structurally foreclosed” our ability to see and act upon humanity crippled by circuits of destruction.[22]

A more compelling conclusion is that looking has become increasingly and overwhelmingly controlled by centralized, corporate visual media outlets. Even nominally alternative outlets for do-it-yourself image makers such as YouTube and Instagram are backed by corporate entities (YouTube was purchased by Google in 2006) or are subsidized according to corporate models (such as Instagram’s and Facebook’s negotiations with advertisers[23]). It is hard to advocate for the value of humanity through images when those images are being valued by corporate interests for their financial profitability. Today, most news outlets are more committed to their bottom line. News that has not been influenced by the interests and censorship of corporate entities has become harder to find. In this the already troubling news adage “if it bleeds, it leads” testifies not simply to the prurient interests of news reader- and viewerships, but also to the relative profitability of human catastrophes.

Nevertheless, small-scale and grassroots documentaries and image archives have developed to provide a kind of counterarchive to the more widespread mainstream visualizations of New Orleans and the Gulf after Katrina. Film scholar Dan Streible credits the online archive Hurricane Digital Memory Bank and the late filmmaker Helen Hill and her New Orleans collaborators with collecting and circulating images and stories developed by local residents.[24] The multilayered collections and documents defy simplistic readings and co-optation by foregrounding the residents’ contributions to the projects and their own contextualizing of the visual artifacts. In his study of Hill and her networks of dissemination, Streible reveals local circuits of production and dissemination that supported, before and after Katrina, a New Orleans–area community practiced in discussing the local political and social environment in cinematic and other visual terms.

In one sense, we can decry the hypermanagement of image distribution networks and mourn the demise of the powerful, game-changing use of images that have been described in this study. But to do so would be to mistake the power of distribution networks for the pathos of the image. We should not mourn for the supposed loss of the image’s power; we should mourn for the loss of the lives and the safety of those individuals whose bodies revealed the depriving of their lives even as they instructed us in ours. It is those lives that resist conscription into easy narratives that regard black lives as necessarily and naturally “bare lives,” to use the language of Georgio Agamben—lives that are always closer to death than those lives that are better represented in systems of power.

Rather, we ought to attend to the humanity of the intimate look epitomized by the loving regard that kin and community are able to bestow upon the wounded and the deceased. Outside of the mainstream circuits of looking codified in mass media outlets and even museum exhibitions, black suffering and death continue to resonate. They register above all with the black kin and black communities of the wounded and deceased. As Karla Holloway reminds us, "[T]he dead and the ways of our dying have been as much a part of black identity as have been the ways of our living," and the spectacle of black pain has come to constitute, Elizabeth Alexander instructs, "a traumatized collective historical memory which is reinvoked . . . at contemporary sites of conflict."[25] Alongside this activation of memories of pain we would do well to "recall as well and rightly [W. E. B.] Du Bois's mournful narrative of parental loss. It harbingers a passing of children, elders and infants, young and middle-aged black folk—each of whom is folded into a national narrative as African American legacy."[26]

Not all losses are made visible to a wider public. Most are guarded by the respectful vigil of those closest who mourn loss as they celebrate life as an extraordinary act of survival. Poet Audre Lorde's reminder that "[w]e were not meant to survive" in her poem "A Litany for Survival" articulates deep truths about the black presence in America.[27] It is a history studded with struggles for the right to bodily integrity and spiritual autonomy. Another African American woman poet, June Jordon, responds to Lorde's call: "Some of us did not die."[28] Jordan's declaration balances a celebration of survival and tribute to those who were cut down, thereby defining the task of living as significantly and productively informed by its witness to pain and death. This balance "has something to do with the fact that all survivors, however they accommodate or fail to remember it, bear the inexorable guilt of the survivor," James Baldwin explains, adding, "It has something to do . . . with having once been a Black child in a White country. My memory stammers, but my soul is a witness."[29]

This is the lucidity that comes with humane insight, a wisdom that understands modes of mourning as forms of activism. It is to these activist-mourners that we should look, if we are not such ourselves, not to offer pallid and superficial consolation but to observe and affirm that human life always matters.

Notes

Acknowledgments

1. Certeau, Michel de, *The Practice of Everyday Life*, trans. Steven F. Rendall (Berkeley: University of California Press, 1984), 91.

2. Ibid., 92.

3. Ibid.

4. Ibid.

Introduction

1. Susan Sontag, *Regarding the Pain of Others* (New York: Farrar, Straus and Giroux, 2003), 42.

2. Sharon Sliwinski, *Human Rights In Camera* (Chicago: University of Chicago Press, 2011), 4–5.

3. Susan Sontag, *On Photography* (New York: Farrar, Straus and Giroux, 1977), 14.

4. Frantz Fanon, *Black Skin, White Masks*, trans. Charles Lam Markmann (New York: Grove Press, 1967; Paris: Seuil, 1952), 112. Page references are to the English edition.

5. Fanon, *Black Skin, White Masks*, 232.

6. Saidiya Hartman, *Scenes of Subjection: Terror, Slavery, and Self-Making in Nineteenth-Century America* (New York: Oxford University Press, 1997), 18.

7. Elizabeth Alexander, "'Can You Be BLACK and Look at This?': Reading the Rodney King Video(s)," in *Black Male: Representations of Masculinity in Contemporary American Art*, ed. Thelma Golden (New York: Whitney Museum of American Art, 1994), 91.

8. Elaine Scarry, *The Body in Pain: The Making and Unmaking of the World* (New York: Oxford University Press, 1985), 34.

9. Scarry, *Body in Pain,* 31.

10. Debra Walker King, *African Americans and the Culture of Pain* (Charlottesville: University of Virginia Press, 2008), 9.

11. Ibid., 9.

12. Ibid., 16.

13. Ibid., 125.

14. Paul Gilroy, *After Empire: Melancholia or Convivial Culture?* (Abingdon, England: Routledge, 2004), 20.

15. Hartman, *Scenes of Subjection,* 5.

16. Emmanuel C. Eze, *Achieving Our Humanity: The Idea of the Postracial Future* (New York: Routledge, 2001), 3.

17. In the texts of Aristotle and continuing to those of Aquinas, the issue is discussed in terms of the human soul. Aristotle, in *de Anima,* explains that it is the soul in combination with the body that defines the human. Analogizing the eye to the body and sight to the soul, Aristotle makes a distinction between tool and essence while demonstrating the contingency of the body to the soul and vice versa. The Aristotle of the *Nichomachean Ethics,* however, changes the terms of his discussion somewhat and considers what constitutes the *good* human being. To account for the moral differentiation implied by the good, Aristotle introduces "the rational principle" and explains that "the function of man [is] . . . an activity or actions of the soul implying a rational principle"; Aristotle, *Nicomachean Ethics,* trans. W. D. Ross (New York: Oxford University Press, 2009), 1098a, lines 12–15. For Aristotle, the soul does not have an overtly religious cast; however, it does for Christian theologian and philosopher Thomas Aquinas. Aquinas radically revises Aristotle's philosophy of the soul by declaring it possible (though not necessary) to separate body from soul. As an "intellectual principle," Aquinas maintains, the soul exceeds the body in its orientation toward knowledge. Where "every body has a determinate nature" (*Summa Theologica* 1. q. 76, art. 1, ad. 2.), the soul has no fixed orientation and remains mutable; Thomas Aquinas, *Summa Theologica: Complete English Edition in Five Volumes,* vol. 4, trans. Fathers of the English Dominican Province (Westminster, MD: Christian Classics, 1981), 370. We can see the implications in Aquinas's philosophy for the linking of reason to the soul: any action or, as Aquinas calls it, exercise of "free-will" on the part of man indicates his capacity for rational thought and is an expression of his soul. Later, the efflorescence of empiricism orients studies of the human away from theology and toward science, but still manages to avoid the materiality of the body. Reason, which figures in Aristotle's and Aquinas's visions of the human as the method by which man becomes good, is loosened from its moral implications in the empiricist philosophy of René Descartes. One can, Descartes reasons, exercise faulty logic. Nevertheless, man's ability to at the very least *attempt* to determine his actions through reason (even if the actions turn out to be "bad") is enough, in his opinion, to constitute what it means to be human. With Descartes's critical revision, the soul, an essence heretofore permanently oriented toward the good, gives way to the more morally neutral "consciousness." Furthermore, Descartes

is one of the earliest contributors to modern accounts of race as he brought man's "rational essence" into conversation with the ontology of the human; Eze, *Achieving Our Humanity,* 12.

18. Louise M. Antony, "'Human Nature' and Its Role in Feminist Theory," in *Philosophy in a Feminist Voice: Critiques and Reconstructions,* ed. Janet A. Kourany (Princeton, NJ: Princeton University Press, 1998), 64.

19. Once a proponent of the concept of human nature in feminist discourse, Louise Antony has since revised her stance to question the usefulness of "nature" as a universalist concept. Her original reasoning, however, remains a useful articulation of the stakes involved in defining the human. Antony phrased her argument thus: "[I]n order to explain what is wrong with patriarchy and to put forward our positive vision of equitable and sustaining human relationships, we need to affirm our humanity"; Louise M. Antony, "Natures and Norms," *Ethics* 111, no. 1 (October 2000): 11. I repeat her words here because they demonstrate the ethical implications for a notion of humanity. Antony's revised stance—"the fact—if it is one—that such human universals as exist are due to our nature as human beings is itself of no ethical importance" (Antony, "Natures and Norms," 12)—helps to further dissociate humanity from human nature, a move that makes clearer my specific interest in African Americans' rhetorical deployment of humanity while acknowledging and explaining their desire to distance themselves from a notion of human nature. This distinction, Antony's argument demonstrates, is not uninformed hypocrisy, but a rather subtle discursive, philosophical, and, above all, necessary revision.

20. For an in-depth study of Darwin's contributions to the definition of human nature, see Carl N. Degler, *In Search of Human Nature: The Decline and Revival of Darwinism in American Social Thought* (New York: Oxford University Press, 1991).

21. Carl Schmitt, *The Concept of the Political,* trans. George Schwab (Chicago: University of Chicago Press, 1996; Tübingen, Germany: Mohr, 1927), 54. Page references are to the English edition.

22. Ibid. (emphasis added).

23. See, for instance, Richard Rorty, *Achieving Our Country: Leftist Thought in Twentieth-Century America* (Cambridge, MA: Harvard University Press, 1998).

24. Martha C. Nussbaum, *Women and Human Development: The Capabilities Approach* (Cambridge: Cambridge University Press, 2000); Amartya Sen, *Commodities and Capabilities* (New York: Oxford University Press, 1999).

25. Gilroy, *After Empire,* 4.

26. Giorgio Agamben, *Homo Sacer: Sovereign Power and Bare Life,* trans. Daniel Heller-Roazen (Stanford: Stanford University Press, 1998).

27. Karla F. C. Holloway, *Passed On: African American Mourning Stories: A Memorial* (Durham, NC: Duke University Press, 2003).

28. I am thinking here of the work of Trinh T. Minh-ha and Dirk Eitzen, to name but two influential theorists of documentary.

29. Nancy Armstrong, *Fiction in the Age of Photography: The Legacy of British Realism* (Cambridge, MA: Harvard University Press, 1999).

Chapter 1. Slavery's Suffering Brought to Light—New Orleans, 1834

1. See Harriet Martineau, *Retrospect of Western Travel,* vol. 1 (New York: Harper and Brothers, 1838), 265; George W. Cable, "The Haunted House in Royal Street," *The Century* 38, no. 4 (August 1889): 594; and "The Negro Race in America," *The Edinburgh Review, or Critical Journal* 119, no. 243 (January 1864): 208.

2. This version of events is reported by author Henry C. Castellanos who wrote in 1895, "Among [the rescued slaves], a woman confessed to the Mayor that she had purposely set fire to the house, as the only means of putting an end to her sufferings and those of her fellow captives." Henry Castellanos, *New Orleans As It Was: Episodes of Louisiana Life,* 2nd ed. (New Orleans: L. Graham and Son, 1905; 1st ed., 1895), 54. Page number references are to the 1905 edition.

3. *New Orleans Bee,* April 11, 1834, morning edition, 2, col. B.

4. On the reliability of these newspaper reports, see Fred R. Darkis Jr., "Madame Lalaurie of New Orleans," *Louisiana History: The Journal of the Louisiana Historical Association* 23, no. 4 (1982): 383–99.

5. From the *Essex Register* as quoted in Boston's *Liberator* 1, no. 30 (May 3, 1834), 71, col. D; from New York's *Journal of Commerce* 8, no. 582 (April 30, 1834), 2, col. B; from the *New Orleans Mercantile Advisor* as quoted in the *Liberator* 1, no. 30 (May 3, 1834), 71, col. B; *New Orleans Bee,* April 11, 1834, morning edition, 2, col. B; "A Horrible Affair," in Baltimore's *Niles' Register* 46 (May 3, 1834), 152; E. Thomas, *A Concise View of the Slavery of the People of Colour in the United States, Exhibiting Some of the Most Affecting Cases of Cruel and Barbarous Treatment of the Slaves by Their Most Inhuman and Brutal Masters, Not Heretofore Published: Also Showing the Absolute Necessity for the Most Speedy Abolition of Slavery, with an Endeavour to Point Out the Best Means of Effecting It* (Philadelphia: E. Thomas, 1834), 32–38.

6. Katherine Helm, *The True Story of Mary, Wife of Lincoln* (New York: Harper, 1928), 38–39.

7. Elaine Scarry, *Dreaming by the Book* (New York: Farrar, Straus and Giroux, 1999), 3.

8. *Liberator,* May 10, 1834.

9. *New Orleans Bee,* April 11, 1834, morning edition, 2, col. A.

10. Though no sufficient explanation has ever been given, Delphine Lalaurie is consistently identified by the news reports as the perpetrator of the abuse.

11. "Facts," *Liberator,* May 10, 1834, 3, col. A.

12. Sally Gomaa, "Writing to 'Virtuous' and 'Gentle' Readers: The Problem of Pain in Harriet Jacobs's *Incidents* and Harriet Wilson's *Sketches,*" *African American Review* 43, no. 2–3 (2011): 375.

13. Jeannine DeLombard, "'Eye-Witness to the Cruelty': Southern Violence and Northern Testimony in Frederick Douglass's 1845 *Narrative,*" *American Literature* 73, no. 2 (2001): 245.

14. Saidiya Hartman, *Scenes of Subjection: Terror, Slavery, and Self-Making in Nineteenth-Century America* (New York: Oxford University Press, 1997), 3.

15. Frederick Douglass, "Letter to Samuel Hanson Cox, D.D. (1846)," in *Frederick Douglass: Selected Speeches and Writings*, ed. Philip S. Foner and Yuval Taylor (Chicago: Lawrence Hill Books, 1999), 47.

16. Ibid., 41.

17. Cox as quoted in Douglass, "Letter," 41.

18. Debra Walker King, *African Americans and the Culture of Pain* (Charlottesville: University of Virginia Press, 2008), 15, 9.

19. Celeste-Marie Bernier, "'Iron Arguments': Spectacle, Rhetoric and the Slave Body in New England and British Antislavery Oratory," *European Journal of American Culture* 26, no.1 (2007): 63.

20. *New Orleans Bee,* April 12, 1834, morning edition, 2, col. A.

21. Castellanos, *New Orleans As It Was,* 54.

22. Barbara J. Shapiro, *Probability and Certainty in Seventeenth-Century England: A Study of the Relationships between Natural Science, Religion, History, Law, and Literature* (Princeton, NJ: Princeton University Press, 1983).

23. Thomas W. Laqueur, "Bodies, Details, and the Humanitarian Narrative," in *The New Cultural History,* ed. Lynn Hunt (Berkeley: University of California Press, 1989), 177.

24. Karen Halttunen, "Humanitarianism and the Pornography of Pain in Anglo-American Culture," *American Historical Review* 100, no. 2 (1995): 303.

25. Margaret N. Abruzzo, *Polemical Pain: Slavery, Cruelty, and the Rise of Humanitarianism* (Baltimore: Johns Hopkins University Press, 2011), 24–25, 50.

26. Halttunen, "Humanitarianism and the Pornography of Pain," 303.

27. Ibid., 307.

28. Ibid., 309.

29. "The eighteenth-century cult of sensibility redefined pain as unacceptable and indeed eradicable and thus opened the door to a new revulsion from pain, which, though later regarded as 'instinctive' or 'natural,' has in fact proved to be distinctly modern." Ibid., 304.

30. Abruzzo, *Polemical Pain,* 6.

31. Alan Trachtenberg, *Reading American Photographs: Images as History, Mathew Brady to Walker Evans* (New York: Hill and Wang, 1989), 53. For more on Agassiz's project, see Elinor Reichlin, "Faces of Slavery," *American Heritage* 28, no. 4 (June 1977): 4–11; Stephen Jay Gould, *The Mismeasure of Man* (New York: Norton, 1996); Brian Wallis, "Black Bodies, White Science: Louis Agassiz's Slave Daguerreotypes," *American Art* 9, no. 2 (Summer 1995): 38–61; Mandy Reid, "Selling Shadows and Substance: Photographing Race in the United States, 1850–1870s," *Early Popular Visual Culture* 4, no. 3 (November 2006): 285–305; and Lee D. Baker, *From Savage to Negro: Anthropology and the Construction of Race, 1896–1954* (Berkeley: University of California Press, 1998).

32. Allan Sekula, "The Traffic in Photographs," *Art Journal* 41, no. 1 (1981): 16.
33. Louis Agassiz as quoted in Wallis, "Black Bodies, White Science," 42.
34. Kyla Schuller, "Taxonomies of Feeling: The Epistemology of Sentimentalism in Late-Nineteenth-Century Racial and Sexual Science," *American Quarterly* 64, no. 2 (2012): 287.
35. Ibid., 286.
36. Hartman, *Scenes of Subjection,* 36.
37. Gomaa, "Writing to 'Virtuous' and 'Gentle' Readers," 371.
38. "My Heart Is Sick," *Liberator* 1, no. 30 (July 23, 1831), 117.
39. Ibid.
40. Ibid.
41. Ibid.
42. "Horrid Cruelty," *Liberator* 1, no. 45 (November 5, 1831), 178.
43. Ibid.
44. "Convention at Lynn," *Liberator,* May 10, 1844, 75, col. D.
45. "New England Anti-Slavery Convention," *Liberator,* June 8, 1855, 90, col. E, and 89, col. F.
46. Gomaa, "Writing to 'Virtuous' and 'Gentle' Readers," 371. I depart somewhat from Gomaa's assertion that "[t]he radical transformation from 'thing' to 'man' was enacted on the abolitionist platform by displaying slaves' bodies *in pain*" (371, emphasis mine) because the person on stage was not necessarily in the throes of physical pain; to the contrary, it seems, if Anthony Burns can supply an example, that the speaker had some distance from the pain if not mastery over it and instead displayed to the audience the physical trace that the painful experience had left behind.
47. Giorgio Agamben, *Homo Sacer: Sovereign Power and Bare Life,* trans. Daniel Heller-Roazen (Stanford, CA: Stanford University Press, 1998).
48. *New Orleans Bee,* April 12, 1843, morning edition, 2, col. A. (Emphasis in the original.)
49. Ibid.
50. Darkis, "Madame Lalaurie of New Orleans," 391.
51. Ibid.
52. Ibid.
53. *Civil Code of the State of Louisiana: With the Statutory Amendments, from 1825 to 1853, inclusive; and References to the Decisions of the Supreme Court of Louisiana to the Sixth Volume of Annual Reports,* ed. Thomas G. Morgan (New Orleans: J. B. Steel, 1857), ch. 3, art. 173, p. 28.
54. William Goodell, *The American Slave Code in Theory and Practice: Its Distinctive Features Shown by Its Statutes, Judicial Decisions, and Illustrative Facts* (New York: American and Foreign Anti-Slavery Society, 1853), 291. (Emphasis in the original.)
55. *New Orleans Bee,* April 12, 1834, morning edition, 2, col. A.
56. George Washington Cable, *Strange True Stories of Louisiana* (New York: C. Scribner's Sons, 1889), 216.

57. *Journal of Commerce,* April 20, 1834.

58. *New Orleans Bee,* April 12, 1834, morning edition, 2, col. A; *Journal of Commerce,* April 20, 1834.

59. *Civil Code of the State of Louisiana,* ch. 2, art. 455.

60. *Civil Code of the State of Louisiana,* ch. 2, art. 462; Judith K. Schafer, "Roman Roots of the Louisiana Law of Slavery: Emancipation in American Louisiana, 1803–1857," *Louisiana Law Review* 56, no. 2 (1995): 417.

61. *New Orleans Bee,* April 12, 1843, morning edition, 2, col. A.

62. James Turner, *Reckoning with the Beast: Animals, Pain, and Humanity in the Victorian Mind* (Baltimore: Johns Hopkins University, 1980), 39–59.

63. Ibid., 44 (emphasis added).

64. *New Orleans Bee,* April 12, 1843, morning edition, 2, col. A.

Chapter 2. Framed and Shamed

1. It is worth pointing out, as many historians have, that the amendment does not actually abolish slavery, but restricts its application to "punishment for crime whereof the party shall have been duly convicted."

2. Leigh Raiford, "Lynching, Visuality, and the Un/Making of Blackness," *Nka: Journal of Contemporary African Art* 20 (Fall 2006): 22.

3. See Amy Louise Wood, *Lynching and Spectacle: Witnessing Racial Violence in America, 1890–1940* (Chapel Hill: University of North Carolina Press, 2009); Koritha Mitchell, *Living with Lynching: African American Lynching Plays, Performance, and Citizenship, 1890–1930* (Urbana: University of Illinois Press, 2011); and Jacqueline Goldsby, *A Spectacular Secret: Lynching in American Life and Literature* (Chicago: University of Chicago Press, 2006).

4. Philip Dray, *At the Hands of Persons Unknown: The Lynching of Black America* (New York: Random House, 2002), 18.

5. Wood, *Lynching and Spectacle,* 8.

6. Ibid., 25.

7. Shawn Michelle Smith, *Photography on the Color Line: W. E. B. Du Bois, Race, and Visual Culture* (Durham, NC: Duke University Press, 2004), 122, 125.

8. See Ida B. Wells, *A Red Record: Tabulated Statistics and Alleged Causes of Lynchings in the United States, 1892–1893–1894* (Chicago: Donohue and Henneberry, 1895); Ida B. Wells-Barnett, *Southern Horrors: Lynch Law in All Its Phases* (New York: New York Age Print, 1892); Ida B. Wells-Barnett, *Southern Horrors and Other Writings: The Anti-Lynching Campaign of Ida B. Wells, 1892–1900,* ed. Jacqueline J. Royster (Boston: Bedford Books, 1997); and Leigh Raiford, *Imprisoned in a Luminous Glare: Photography and the African American Freedom Struggle* (Chapel Hill: University of North Carolina Press, 2011), 43.

9. Wood, *Lynching and Spectacle,* 205.

10. Ibid., 206.

11. Fredric Jameson, "Postmodernism, or the Cultural Logic of Late Capitalism," *New Left Review* 146 (1984): 59.

12. Daniel J. Sherman and Irit Rogoff, "Introduction: Frameworks for Critical Analysis," in *Museum Culture: Histories, Discourses, Spectacles,* ed. Daniel J. Sherman and Irit Rogoff (Minneapolis: University of Minnesota Press, 1994), xii.

13. Mitchell, *Living with Lynching,* 1.

14. Antilynching pamphlet (1935), part 7, series A, reel 9, NAACP Papers. See also Wood, *Lynching and Spectacle.*

15. White had experienced the terrorism of lynching firsthand. In the chapter of his autobiography titled "I Decline to Be Lynched," White describes how he narrowly escaped being the victim of a lynching during the Elaine race riot, Arkansas. When it was uncovered that White, who had been reporting on the riot for the *Chicago Daily News,* was black (he had been passing for white to gain access for his report), White fled for his life by boarding the next train to Little Rock. The conductor, unaware that White was the man being sought, informed him that it was unfortunate that he was leaving "just when the fun [was] going to start" because "[t]here's a damned yellow nigger passing for white and the boys are going to get him." Asked what would happen to the man were he caught, the conductor replied, "When they get through with him he won't pass for white no more!" When White reached Memphis later that day, he wrote that "the news had been circulated that I had been lynched in Arkansas that afternoon." Walter White, *A Man Called White: The Autobiography of Walter White* (Athens: University of Georgia Press, 1995; New York: Viking Press, 1948), 51. Page number references are to the 1995 edition.

16. Walter Francis White, letter to Gertrude Vanderbilt Whitney, December 13, 1934 (Fredericksburg, MD: Papers of the NAACP).

17. Ibid.

18. Walter Francis White, letter to Suzanne La Follette, December 13, 1934 (Fredericksburg, MD: Papers of the NAACP). (Emphasis in the original.)

19. W. E. B. DuBois, "Criteria of Negro Art" (1926), in *African American Literary Theory: A Reader,* ed. Winston Napier (New York: New York University Press, 2000), 22.

20. This exhibition, called *Struggle for Negro Rights,* opened on March 2, 1935, at the American Contemporary Art Gallery in Greenwich Village, New York, and ran until March 16. It was sponsored by members of the Artists' Union, the League of Struggle for Negro Rights, the Vanguard Group, the John Reed Club, and the International Labor Defense. Dora Apel, *Imagery of Lynching: Black Men, White Women, and the Mob* (New Brunswick, NJ: Rutgers University Press, 2004), 84.

21. See Dora Apel's analysis of this and the contemporaneous antilynching show held by the Communist Party in the chapter titled "The Antilynching Exhibitions of 1935: Strategies and Constraints" in her book *Imagery of Lynching.*

22. Ibid., 90.

23. Ibid., 88.

24. Ibid., 90.

25. Margaretta M. Salinger, "Current Exhibitions [Review of *An Art Commentary on Lynching*]," *Parnassus* 7, no. 3 (March 1935): 24.

26. M. M., "Art Commentary on Lynching," *Art News* 33 (February 23, 1935): 13.

27. Winsten's obituary in the *New York Times* declared, in part, "Mr. Winsten took a no-nonsense, meat and potatoes approach to his work, telling readers what he felt they would want to know in deciding whether they would enjoy a movie and making no effort to assess its artistic merit." Robert McG. Thomas Jr., "Archer Winsten, 92, Movie Reviewer at *The Post,* Dies [Obituary (Obit)]," *New York Times,* February 23, 1997, late edition (East Coast), sec. 1, 39.

28. Archer Winsten, "Art Goes Educational on Decorous East Fifty-Seventh, near Fifth," *New York Post,* February 18, 1935, n.p.

29. Ibid.

30. Trudier Harris, *Exorcising Blackness: Historical and Literary Lynching and Burning Rituals* (Bloomington: Indiana University Press, 1984), 5–6. See also Robyn Wiegman, "The Anatomy of Lynching," *Journal of the History of Sexuality* 3, no. 3 (January 1993): 445–67.

31. Buck as quoted in Winsten, "Art Goes Educational," n.p.

32. Winsten, "Art Goes Educational," n.p.

33. Newton as quoted in Winsten, "Art Goes Educational," n.p.

34. Winsten, "Art Goes Educational," n.p.

35. See James Allen, *Without Sanctuary: Lynching Photography in America* (Santa Fe, NM: Twin Palms, 2000).

36. This configuration entailed the inclusion of other artifacts, including books, clothing, posters, and music related to lynching.

37. For a review of the show with a thorough description of the exhibition hall, see Duane J. Corpis and Ian Christopher Fletcher, "Without Sanctuary," *Radical History Review* 85 (2003): 282–85.

38. Apel, *Imagery of Lynching,* 11, 12–13.

39. See Robert L. Zangrando, *The NAACP Crusade against Lynching, 1909–1950* (Philadelphia: Temple University Press, 1980); and Ida B. Wells-Barnett, *On Lynchings: Southern Horrors, A Red Record, Mob Rule in New Orleans* (New York: Arno Press and the *New York Times,* 1969).

40. Daryl White, "Museum and Exhibit Reviews: Without Sanctuary: Lynching in America," *Public Historian* 25, no. 1 (2003): 123; Adam Lynch, "'Without Sanctuary' Exhibit Details Horror of Lynchings," *Mississippi Link,* February 11, 2004, sec. A, 1.

41. Danny Postel, "A Photography Exhibition Unearths the Painful History of Lynching in America," *Chronicle of Higher Education* 48, no. 44 (July 12, 2003), A14.

42. Ibid.

43. "Death by Lynching," *New York Times,* March 16, 2000, A22.

44. Susan Sontag, *Regarding the Pain of Others* (New York: Farrar, Straus and Giroux, 2003), 120.

45. Karen Dumas, "Still, without Sanctuary," *Michigan Chronicle,* September 14, 2004, A6.

46. For more on black-white looking relations, see Jane M. Gaines, "White Privilege and Looking Relations: Race and Gender in Feminist Film Theory," *Screen* 29, no. 4 (1988): 12–27; and bell hooks, *Black Looks: Race and Representation* (Boston: South End Press, 1992).

47. These series of images are from the lynching of Frank Embree (catalog numbers 42, 43, and 44) and the lynching of Will James (catalog numbers 45–52) in Allen's *Without Sanctuary* catalog.

48. Allen, *Without Sanctuary,* 181.

49. Allen, *Without Sanctuary,* 181; Henry Louis Gates Jr., "The Face and Voice of Blackness," in *Facing History: The Black Image in American Art, 1710—1940,* ed. Guy C. McElroy (San Francisco: Bedford Arts, 1990), xxix; Smith, *Photography on the Color Line,* 44.

50. Roberta Smith, "An Ugly Legacy Lives On, Its Glare Unsoftened by Age," *New York Times,* January 13, 2000, 8.

51. Ibid.

52. Maurice O. Wallace, *Constructing the Black Masculine: Identity and Ideality in African American Men's Literature and Culture, 1775–1995* (Durham, NC: Duke University Press, 2002), 19–20. (Emphasis in the original.)

53. José Muñoz, *Disidentifications: Queers of Color and the Performance of Politics* (Minneapolis: University of Minnesota Press, 1999), 4.

54. Michael Hallett, "Commerce with Criminals: The New Colonialism in Criminal Justice," *Review of Policy Research* 21, no. 1 (2004): 51 (emphasis added).

55. Sontag, *Regarding the Pain of Others,* 121.

56. Carrie Rentschler, "Witnessing: US Citizenship and the Vicarious Experience of Suffering," *Media, Culture, and Society* 26, no. 2 (2004): 301.

57. Leon Litwack, "Hellhounds," in Allen, *Without Sanctuary,* 33–34.

58. Thomas Scheff, *Bloody Revenge: Emotions, Nationalism, and War* (Boulder, CO: Westview Press, 1994), 51. (Emphasis in the original.)

59. Eve Sedgwick and Adam Frank, "Shame in the Cybernetic Fold: Reading Silvan Tomkins," *Critical Inquiry* 21 (1995): 520.

60. Elspeth Probyn, *Blush: Faces of Shame* (Minneapolis: University of Minnesota Press, 2005), 49, 39.

61. Ibid., 56.

62. Sontag, *Regarding the Pain of Others,* 119.

63. Certainly one must acknowledge, thanks to Deborah Willis (*J. P. Ball: Daguerrean and Studio Photographer,* ed. Deborah Willis [New York: Garland, 1993]), that at least one photographer of lynching scenes was black: J. P. Ball, who on at least one occasion agitated against one black man's lynching (Goldsby, *Spectacular Secret,* 246). Jacqueline Goldsby, whose book looks at the representation of lynching as a public secret in the writing of Ida B. Wells, James Weldon Johnson, and others, explains in

her caption to one of Ball's photographs the distinctness of African American photographers of lynching: "African American photographers did not shy away from making lynching photographs but often did so by fashioning them into framed narratives. Juxtaposing photographs of the murder scene with images of the victim alive or lying in state at his funeral, these series establish ethical boundaries within which looking at the murder becomes a point of interest" (Goldsby, *Spectacular Secret,* 244). This is arguably what happened in the wake of Emmett Till's funeral, which is discussed in chapter 3.

Chapter 3. Emmett Till, Justice, and the Task of Recognition

1. This précis is culled from several newspaper accounts, most of which are collected in the anthology *The Lynching of Emmett Till: A Documentary Narrative,* ed. Christopher Metress (Charlottesville: University of Virginia Press, 2002).

2. Mamie [Till-Mobley] Bradley speech in South Bend, Indiana, in 1955, quoted in Clenora Hudson-Weems, *Emmett Till: The Sacrificial Lamb of the Civil Rights Movement* (Troy, MI: Bedford Publishers, 2000), 300.

3. Mamie Till-Mobley and Christopher Benson, *Death of Innocence: The Story of the Hate Crime That Changed America* (New York: Random House, 2003), 131.

4. Ibid., 133. The 2006 report of the Federal Bureau of Investigation, a product of their reopening of the case in 2005, includes statements from the black Mississippi undertaker Chester Miller and an unnamed witness that seem to contradict Mamie Till's assertion. These documents claim that upon learning that the body was to be shipped to Chicago, the unnamed witness "and Chester Miller went to the funeral home in Tutwiler [whence the body had been removed after discovery] and were told they [the Tutwiler funeral home employees] had soaked the body in fluid to preserve it. The body was placed in rubber pouches, placed in a casket and [Miller and the witness] took the body to Clarksdale to the train." Federal Bureau of Investigation, *Prosecutive Report of Investigation Concerning [Redacted]; [Redacted]; Roy Bryant—Deceased; John William Milam, also known as J. W. Milam—Deceased; Leslie F. Milam—Deceased; Melvin L. Campbell—Deceased; Elmer O. Kimbrell—Deceased; Hubert Clark—Deceased; Levi Colins, also known as Too Tight Collins—Deceased; Johnny B. Washington—Deceased; Otha Johnson Jr., also known as Oso—Deceased; [redacted]; Emmett Louis Till—Deceased—Victim; Civil Rights—Conspiracy; Domestic Police Cooperation* (Washington, DC: Federal Bureau of Investigation, 2006), 81.

5. Till-Mobley and Benson, *Death of Innocence,* 133.

6. Jacques Derrida, *Specters of Marx: The State of the Debt, the Work of Mourning, and the New International* (New York: Routledge, 1994), 9. (Emphasis in the original.)

7. Hudson-Weems, *Emmett Till,* 302.

8. Till-Mobley and Benson, *Death of Innocence,* 135–36.

9. Ibid., 134.

10. Jacques Lacan, "The Mirror Stage as Formative of the *I* Function [1949]," in *Écrits: A Selection*, trans. Bruce Fink (New York: W. W. Norton, 2002), 4.

11. Jessica Benjamin, *The Bonds of Love: Psychoanalysis, Feminism, and the Problem of Domination* (New York: Pantheon, 1988), 16.

12. Ibid., 21.

13. Ibid., 21.

14. Till-Mobley and Benson, *Death of Innocence*, 134–35. (Emphasis in the original.)

15. Elaine Scarry, *The Body in Pain: The Making and Unmaking of the World* (New York: Oxford University Press, 1985), 36.

16. Till-Mobley and Benson, *Death of Innocence*, 190.

17. On the repression of the emotions of the enslaved, see Saidiya Hartman, *Scenes of Subjection: Terror, Slavery, and Self-Making in Nineteenth-Century America* (New York: Oxford University Press, 1997).

18. Till-Mobley and Benson, *Death of Innocence*, 129.

19. Bradley speech in South Bend, Indiana, in 1955, as quoted in Hudson-Weems, *Emmett Till*, 304.

20. Till-Mobley and Benson, *Death of Innocence*, 142.

21. Ibid., 139. (Emphasis in the original.)

22. Stanley B. Burns, *Sleeping Beauty: Memorial Photography in America* (Altadena, CA: Twelvetrees Press, 1990), n.p.

23. Ibid., n.p.

24. Till-Mobley and Benson, *Death of Innocence*, 159.

25. Elizabeth Alexander, "'Can You Be BLACK and Look at This?': Reading the Rodney King Video(s)," in *Black Male: Representations of Masculinity in Contemporary American Art*, ed. Thelma Golden (New York: Whitney Museum of American Art, 1994), 97.

26. Derrida, *Specters of Marx*, xviii.

27. Ibid., xviii–xix (emphasis in the original); Achille Mbembe, "Necropolitics," trans. Libby Meintjes, *Public Culture* 15, no. 1 (2003): 40. (Emphasis in the original.)

28. Karla F. C. Holloway, *Passed On: African American Mourning Stories: A Memorial* (Durham, NC: Duke University Press, 2003), 16. (Emphasis in the original.)

29. Ibid., 27.

30. Alexander, "'Can You Be BLACK and Look at This?'" 91.

31. Alexander notes, "The caption of the close-up photograph of Till's face read: 'Mutilated face of victim was left unretouched by mortician at the mother's request. She said she wanted "all the world" to witness the atrocity.'" Ibid., 102.

32. Ashraf Rushdy, "Exquisite Corpse," *Transition* 9, no. 3 (2000): 70.

33. Ibid. (emphasis added).

34. Robin D. G. Kelley, "'We Are Not What We Seem': Rethinking Black Working-Class Opposition in the Jim Crow South," *Journal of American History* 80, no. 1 (1993): 82.

35. Ibid.

36. I invoke here the word *moved* in the sense outlined by Jane Gaines in her discussion of the relationship between documentary and activism. "By *moved*," she writes, "I mean the mix of affect and action that the double meaning of the word implies. I mean everything from it 'troubled' or 'disturbed' or 'shocked,' to it made you 'get up and do something.'" Jane Gaines, "Radical Attractions: The Uprising of '34," *Wide Angle* 21, no. 2 (1999): 109.

37. Muhammad Ali and Richard Durham, *The Greatest, My Own Story* (New York: Random House, 1975), 34–35.

38. Kareem Abdul-Jabbar and Mignon McCarthy, *Kareem* (New York: Random House, 1990), 205.

39. Derrida, *Specters of Marx*, xx.

40. Testimony of Mamie [Till-Mobley] Bradley, *Official Transcript of State of Mississippi v. J. W. Milam and Roy Bryant*, Seventeenth Judicial District of the State, September 19, 1955, pp. 185–86, 197–205, and 210–12. This trial transcript is appended to the FBI *Prosecutive Report* as appendix A. All citations of the trial transcript derive from this source.

41. Testimony of H. C. Strider, *Official Transcript of State of Mississippi v. J. W. Milam and Roy Bryant*, Seventeenth Judicial District of the State, September 19, 1955, p. 308.

42. Murray Kempton, "2 Face Trial as 'Whistle' Kidnapers—Due to Post Bond and Go Home [1955]," in Metress, *Lynching of Emmett Till*, 108.

43. Sam Johnson [AP correspondent], "Jury Hears Defense and Prosecution Arguments as Testimony Ends in Kidnap-Slaying Case [1955]," in Metress, *Lynching of Emmett Till*, 100. Alas, the closing arguments were not recovered by the FBI and appear to have gone missing before 1962. See Shaila Dewan and Ariel Hart, "F.B.I. Discovers Trial Transcript in Emmett Till Case," *New York Times*, May 18, 2005, A14.

44. Testimony of George Smith, *Official Transcript of State of Mississippi v. J. W. Milam and Roy Bryant*, Seventeenth Judicial District of the State, September 19, 1955, p. 170. As documented in the 2005 FBI report, an autopsy performed on Emmett Till's exhumed remains on June 2, 2005, led to the medical examiner's official opinion that "Emmett Louis Till died of a gunshot wound of the head." *Prosecutive Report*, 110.

45. Testimony of Jon Ed Cothran, *Official Transcript of State of Mississippi v. J. W. Milam and Roy Bryant*, Seventeenth Judicial District of the State, September 19, 1955, pp. 43–44. See also Ralph Hutto, "Mother, 'Surprise Witness' Give Dramatic Testimony: Mamie Bradley Says Corpse Was That of Her Slain Son [part 2, 1955]," in Metress, *Lynching of Emmett Till*, 77, 78.

46. Testimony of H. C. Strider, *Official Transcript of State of Mississippi v. J. W. Milam and Roy Bryant*, Seventeenth Judicial District of the State, September 19, 1955, p. 290.

47. Ibid., p. 291. See also "Sheriff Strider's Testimony Raises Doubt Body in River Was Till Youth," *Jackson Daily News*, September 23, 1955, in Metress, *Lynching of Emmett Till*, 99.

48. After facing criticism, his revised cheerful salutation to Mamie Till and her entourage was, "Mornin,' niggahs." Till-Mobley and Benson, *Death of Innocence*, 165.

49. Smith notes, "Lynching postcards fell under section 3893 of the Revised Statutes which forbid 'lewd, obscene, and lascivious' materials to be sent through the mail." Shawn Michelle Smith, *Photography on the Color Line: W. E. B. Du Bois, Race, and Visual Culture* (Durham: Duke University Press, 2004), 197, n. 30.

50. "Sheriff Strider's Testimony Raises Doubt Body in River Was Till Youth," in Metress, *Lynching of Emmett Till*, 98.

51. Their guilt is certain. After the trial, Bryant and Milam took advantage of the "double jeopardy" rule that prevented them from being tried again and sold the story of their murder to a reporter who published two articles for *Look* magazine: William Bradford Huie, "The Shocking Story of Approved Killing in Mississippi," *Look*, January 24, 1956, 46–48, 50; and William Bradford Huie, "What's Happened to the Emmett Till Killers?," *Look*, January 22, 1957, 63–66, 68.

52. John Herbers, "Jury Selection Reveals Death Demand Unlikely [1955]," in Metress, *Lynching of Emmett Till*, 46.

Chapter 4. Civil Rights and Battered Bodies

1. See Leigh Raiford, *Imprisoned in a Luminous Glare: Photography and the African American Freedom Struggle* (Chapel Hill: University of North Carolina Press, 2011), 67–128, on SNCC's use of photography. See also Sasha Torres, *Black, White, and in Color: Television and Black Civil Rights* (Princeton, NJ: Princeton University Press, 2003), 20–23, for a description of the television market during the civil rights period.

2. Torres, *Black, White, and in Color*, 15.

3. Martin Luther King Jr., "Letter from a Birmingham Jail," in *Why We Can't Wait* (New York: Harper & Row, 1964; Boston: Beacon Press, 2010), 89. Page references are to the 2010 edition. (Emphasis in the original.)

4. Seth Cagin and Philip Dray, *We Are Not Afraid: The Story of Goodman, Schwerner, and Chaney and the Civil Rights Campaign for Mississippi* (New York: Macmillan, 1988), 69.

5. Ibid.

6. Torres, *Black, White, and in Color*, 36–47.

7. For a critical reading of the NBC documentary "Sit-In," see Torres, "The Double Life of 'Sit-In,'" in *Black, White, and in Color*, 36–47. Torres argues that the documentary's retrospective point of view and its narrative identification with reporter Chet Huntley conspire, along with other cinematic elements, to construct a narrative of inevitability in which the civil rights movement stands unquestionably on the side of right.

8. Torres, *Black, White, and in Color*, 39–40.

9. Of course, there were numerous whites involved in the movement, but their involvement in the cause effectively "blackened" them in the terms of the debate and certainly in the eyes of their foes. As black Mississippi lawyer J. Res Brown told

SNCC volunteers during the summer of 1964, "You're going to be classified into two groups in Mississippi: niggers and nigger-lovers, and they're tougher on nigger-lovers." Brown quoted in Cagin and Dray, *We Are Not Afraid*, 31.

10. Bernhard Giesen, "Performing the Sacred: A Durkheimian Perspective on the Performative Turn in the Social Sciences," in *Social Performance: Symbolic Action, Cultural Pragmatics, and Ritual*, ed. Jeffrey C. Alexander, Bernhard Giesen, and Jason L. Mast (Cambridge: Cambridge University Press, 2006), 337.

11. Jack Gould, "'N.B.C. White Paper' on Nashville Issue Is an Exciting Social Document," *New York Times*, December 21, 1960, 62.

12. Ibid.

13. Torres, *Black, White, and in Color*, 3.

14. Ron Eyerman, "Performing Opposition or, How Social Movements Move," in Alexander, Giesen, and Mast, *Social Performance*, 197.

15. Martin Luther King Jr., "Nonviolence and Racial Justice," *Friends Journal* 4, no. 28 (July 26, 1958): 443.

16. King's oft-repeated famous declaration, that "[t]he moral arc of the universe is long, but it bends toward justice," derives from a passage by nineteenth-century American theologian Theodore Parker: "I do not pretend to understand the moral universe; the arc is a long one, my eye reaches but little ways; I cannot calculate the curve and complete the figure by the experience of sight; I can divine it by conscience. And from what I see I am sure it bends towards justice" (84–85). Theodore Parker, "Of Justice and the Conscience," in *Ten Sermons of Religion* (Boston: Crosby, Nichols, 1853), 66–101.

17. Campbell Gibson and Kay Jung, *Historical Census Statistics on Population Totals by Race, 1790 to 1990, and by Hispanic Origin, 1970 to 1990, for the United States, Regions, Divisions, and States*, Working Paper Series no. 56 (Washington, DC: US Census Bureau, 2002), 29.

18. Danny Lyon, *Memories of the Southern Civil Rights Movement* (Chapel Hill: University of North Carolina Press, 1992), 12.

19. Bernard Lafayette as quoted in David E. Sumner, "Nashville, Nonviolence, and the Newspapers: The Convergence of Social Goals with News Values," *Howard Journal of Communications* 6 (October 1995): 102.

20. See the chapter "Come Let Us Build a New World Together" in Leigh Raiford's *Imprisoned in a Luminous Glare* for a discussion of SNCC's press corps. See also Maurice Berger's *For All the World to See: Visual Culture and the Struggle for Civil Rights* (New Haven, CT: Yale University Press, 2010); and Danny Lyon's *Memories of the Southern Civil Rights Movement*.

21. Torres, *Black, White, and in Color*, 35.

22. See Susan Sontag, *On Photography* (New York: Farrar, Straus and Giroux, 1977); and *Regarding the Pain of Others* (New York: Farrar, Straus and Giroux, 2003).

23. Sharon Sliwinski, *Human Rights In Camera* (Chicago: Chicago University Press, 2011), 23.

24. Ibid.

25. Benedict Anderson, *Imagined Communities: Reflections on the Origin and Spread of Nationalism* (London: Verso, 1991), 48, 18.

26. Ibid., 65.

27. Norman Ritter, "Bloody Beatings, a Burning Bus in the South: 'Suddenly a Wild Mob of Toughs Took Over the Unpoliced Depot,'" *Life* 50, no. 21 (May 26, 1961): 22–25.

28. The murder of the white northern Jewish activists Michael Schwerner and Andrew Goodman alongside black southern activist James Chaney in June 1964 has frequently been cited as the most explicit evidence of the segregationist South's color-blind offensive.

29. For a discussion of the negotiations between the White House and Alabama officials, see Raymond Arsenault, *Freedom Riders: 1961 and the Struggle for Racial Justice* (New York: Oxford University Press, 2006); and Taylor Branch, *Parting the Waters: America in the King Years, 1954–63* (New York: Simon and Schuster, 1988).

30. Torres, *Black, White, and in Color,* 24.

31. Ron Eyerman, "Performing Opposition," 193.

32. Sliwinski, *Human Rights In Camera,* 5.

33. James Boylan, "Birmingham: Newspapers in a Crisis," *Columbia Journalism Review* 2, no. 2 (Summer 1963): 30.

34. Lyon, *Memories of the Southern Civil Rights Movement,* 62.

35. Ibid.

36. Martin A. Berger, *Seeing through Race: A Reinterpretation of Civil Rights Photography* (Berkeley: University of California Press, 2011), 4.

37. Arthur M. Schlesinger Jr., *A Thousand Days: John F. Kennedy in the White House* (Boston: Houghton Mifflin, 1965), 960. Kennedy was not the only person to interpret the civil rights movement as the product of white racists. In an opinion column for the *Atlanta Constitution,* reporter Bruce Galphin commented that "in Birmingham, Dr. King and his cause were fortunate enough to have Bull Connor—and television." Bruce Galphin, "'Non,' but Is It 'Un'?," *Atlanta Constitution,* January 8, 1968, n.p.

38. Eric Sevareid, "Negroes Are Bound to Win Their Cause, Which Will Soon Dominate U.S. Politics," *Toledo Blade,* May 12, 1963, sec. 2, 4.

Chapter 5. A Litany for New Orleans, 2005

1. Henry Giroux, "Reading Hurricane Katrina: Race, Class, and the Biopolitics of Disposability," *College Literature* 33, no. 3 (2006): 172–73.

2. Ray Nagin, interview by Garland Robinette, WWL-AM (New Orleans), September 2, 2005.

3. bell hooks, "In Our Glory: Photography and Black Life," in *Picturing Us: African American Identity in Photography,* ed. Deborah Willis (New York: New Press, 1994), 47.

4. Aric Mayer, "Aesthetics of Catastrophe," *Public Culture* 20, no. 2 (2008): 178.

5. For an in-depth discussion of the structural problems that led to the Katrina disaster, see *What Lies Beneath: Katrina, Race, and the State of the Nation*, ed. The South End Press Collective (Cambridge, MA: South End Press, 2007).

6. The Common Ground Health Clinic, the People's Hurricane Relief Fund, and the work of local New Orleans community members such as Malik Rahim and Cherice Harrison-Nelson are examples of effective, community-based aid work.

7. Alisa Bierriea, Mayaba Liebenthal, and Incite! Women of Color against Violence, "To Render Ourselves Visible: Women of Color Organizing and Hurricane Katrina," in the South End Press Collective, *What Lies Beneath*, 41.

8. M. Justin Davis and T. Nathaniel French, "Blaming Victims and Survivors: An Analysis of Post-Katrina Print News Coverage," *Southern Communication Journal* 73, no. 3 (2008): 249.

9. Ibid., 251.

10. A cursory glance at immigration debates and the discourse on captured enemy combatants such as those who have been indefinitely contained at Guantanamo reveals that in the United States, the protection of human rights has contracted so as to protect only documented US citizens. The significance of Katrina lies in its exposing even that distinction to be false.

11. Cheryl I. Harris and Devon W. Carbado, "Perceiving the Image, Framing Identity, and Critiquing 'Crime': Loot or Find: Fact or Frame?" in *After the Storm: Black Intellectuals Explore the Meaning of Hurricane Katrina*, ed. David D. Troutt (New York: New Press, 2006), 97.

12. Joy James, "Political Literacy and Voice," in Troutt, *After the Storm*, 159.

13. For analysis of the Associated Press's inconsistent use of the terms *looting* and *finding* in photo captions, see Harris and Carbado, "Perceiving the Image," 97.

14. "Life Inside the New Orleans Convention Center; Interview with New Orleans Police Superintendent," transcript of interview by Paula Zahn, *Paula Zahn Now*, CNN, September 8, 2005, http://transcripts.cnn.com/TRANSCRIPTS/0509/08/pzn.01.html.

15. Anna Hartnell, "Katrina Tourism and a Tale of Two Cities: Visualizing Race and Class in New Orleans," *American Quarterly* 61, no. 3 (2009): 724.

16. Gray Line Tours, http://www.graylineneworleans.com/hurricane-katrina-tour.html.

17. Bierriea, Liebenthal, and Incite!, "To Render Ourselves Visible," 32.

18. Roland Barthes, *Camera Lucida: Reflections on Photography*, trans. Richard Howard (Paris: Éditions du Seuil, 1980; New York: Hill and Wang, 1981), 92. Page references are to the translated edition.

19. Peggy Phelan, "Francesca Woodman's Photography: Death and the Image One More Time," *Signs* 27, no. 4 (2002): 993–95.

20. Tiffany Brown, "Wade in the Water," in Troutt, *After the Storm*, 49.

21. David Dennis, "Why Isn't New Orleans Mother's Day Parade Shooting a 'National Tragedy'?," *The (UK) Guardian*, May 15, 2013, http://www.theguardian.com/commentisfree/2013/may/15/new-orleans-shooting-not-national-news.

22. Jared Sexton, "The Obscurity of Black Suffering," in Troutt, *After the Storm,* 124. In the essay, Sexton argues that our account of the disaster has been impoverished by an insufficiently probative look that has not seen the extent of racial and economic impact.

23. Users of Facebook and Instagram have, to varying degrees of success, pushed back against these companies' attempts to fully capitulate to corporations seeking to use these programs for marketing purposes. That said, it remains clear that the social networking functions of Facebook and Instagram are underwritten by profit and corporate interests. Cotton Delo, "Instagram's New Feature Lets Brands 'Tag' Consumers in Photo Stream," *AdAge* (May 2, 2013), http://adage.com/article/digital/instagram-introduces-facebook-photo-tagging/241268/.

24. See Dan Streible, "Media Artists, Local Activists, and Outsider Archivists: The Case of Helen Hill," in *Old and New Media after Katrina,* ed. Diane Negra (New York: Palgrave, 2010), 149–74.

25. Karla F. C. Holloway, *Passed On: African American Mourning Stories: A Memorial* (Durham, NC: Duke University Press, 2003), 8; Elizabeth Alexander, "'Can You Be Black and Look at This?': Reading the Rodney King Video(s)," in *Black Male: Representations of Masculinity in Contemporary American Art*, ed. Thelma Golden (New York: Whitney Museum of Modern Art, 1994), 93.

26. Holloway, *Passed On,* 7.

27. Audre Lorde, "A Litany for Survival," in *The Black Unicorn*, collected in *The Collected Poems of Audre Lorde* (New York: Norton, 1997), 255.

28. June Jordan, "Introduction: Some of Us Did Not Die," in *Some of Us Did Not Die: New and Selected Essays of June Jordan* (New York: Basic/Civitas Books, 2002), 3–15.

29. James Baldwin, *The Evidence of Things Not Seen* (New York: Henry Holt, 1985), xiii.

Index

Note: Page numbers in italic refer to illustrations.

COURTNEY R. BAKER is associate professor of American Studies and Black Studies at Occidental College.

THE NEW BLACK STUDIES SERIES

Beyond Bondage: Free Women of Color in the Americas
Edited by David Barry Gaspar and Darlene Clark Hine
The Early Black History Movement, Carter G. Woodson, and Lorenzo Johnston Greene
Pero Gaglo Dagbovie
"Baad Bitches" and Sassy Supermamas: Black Power Action Films *Stephane Dunn*
Black Maverick: T. R. M. Howard's Fight for Civil Rights and Economic Power
David T. Beito and Linda Royster Beito
Beyond the Black Lady: Sexuality and the New African American Middle Class
Lisa B. Thompson
Extending the Diaspora: New Histories of Black People
Dawne Y. Curry, Eric D. Duke, and Marshanda A. Smith
Activist Sentiments: Reading Black Women in the Nineteenth Century
P. Gabrielle Foreman
Black Europe and the African Diaspora *Edited by Darlene Clark Hine, Trica Danielle Keaton, and Stephen Small*
Freeing Charles: The Struggle to Free a Slave on the Eve of the Civil War
Scott Christianson
African American History Reconsidered *Pero Gaglo Dagbovie*
Freud Upside Down: African American Literature and Psychoanalytic Culture
Badia Sahar Ahad
A. Philip Randolph and the Struggle for Civil Rights *Cornelius L. Bynum*
Queer Pollen: White Seduction, Black Male Homosexuality, and the Cinematic
David A. Gerstner
The Rise of Chicago's Black Metropolis, 1920—1929 *Christopher Robert Reed*
Living with Lynching: African American Lynching Plays, Performance, and Citizenship, 1890—1930 *Koritha Mitchell*
Africans to Spanish America: Expanding the Diaspora *Edited by Sherwin K. Bryant, Rachel Sarah O'Toole, & Ben Vinson III*
Rebels and Runaways: Slave Resistance in Nineteenth-Century Florida
Larry Eugene Rivers
The Black Chicago Renaissance *Edited by Darlene Clark Hine and John McCluskey Jr.*
The Negro in Illinois: The WPA Papers *Edited by Brian Dolinar*
Along the Streets of Bronzeville: Black Chicago's Literary Landscape
Elizabeth Schlabach
Gendered Resistance: Women, Slavery, and the Legacy of Margaret Garner
Edited by Mary E. Fredrickson and Delores M. Walters
Racial Blackness and the Discontinuity of Western Modernity *Lindon Barrett, edited by Justin A. Joyce, Dwight A. McBride, and John Carlos Rowe*
Fannie Barrier Williams: Crossing the Borders of Region and Race
Wanda A. Hendricks

The Pekin: The Rise and Fall of Chicago's First Black-Owned Theater
Thomas Bauman
Grounds of Engagement: Apartheid-Era African American and South African Writing
Stéphane Robolin
Humane Insight: Looking at Images of African American Suffering and Death
Courtney R. Baker

The University of Illinois Press
is a founding member of the
Association of American University Presses.

University of Illinois Press
1325 South Oak Street
Champaign, IL 61820-6903
www.press.uillinois.edu